HOME
BAR

HOME BAR

Andy Clarke

OH EDITIONS

CONTENTS

ONE

Classics

TWO

Twists

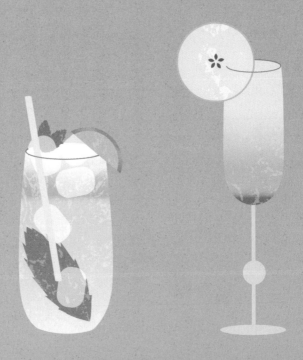

THREE

Batch

78

FOUR

Seasonal

108

FIVE

Cocktail-Time Snacks

134

A HISTORY OF

In a corner of every home is an area where bottles lurk. For some, it's a plinth of pride where beautifully polished spirits stand proud, confidently displaying their shapely curves for all to see. For others, it's a dark, mysterious nook where bottles are hidden from view, seemingly hiding their heads in shame, under a layer of dust, feeling unloved. This area is called 'The Home Bar' and it's a treasure chest full of liquid promise, waiting to be unlocked.

The history of the home bar is interesting. Whilst for centuries the houses of rich families had areas where drinks were fixed by servants, it wasn't until the 1940s that having a home bar was something that became popular. As troops returned home after the Second World War, there was a desire to create bar areas in suburban homes, particularly in the USA. The calm

after the storm created a positivity that manifested itself in celebratory drinking at home. Sometimes these bars would be in the communal areas of the home itself, but often they would be set up in outhouses, sheds and basements.

During the 1950s and 60s, the popularity of the home bar progressed as cabinets, cubbyholes and cupboards proved the popular choice of families across the globe to store and serve their drinks. As a child in the 1980s, I remember a sideboard unit that had a flip-out bar area where drinks were fixed with illuminated mirrored cupboards where spirits, sherry, advocaat and maraschino (cocktail) cherries were stored. It was an Aladdin's cave of imbibement.

THE HOME BAR

Whilst social drinking away from home – in pubs, bars and clubs proved popular in the 1970s, 80s and 90s – at the turn of the 21st century, home drinking became more popular and more creative. Higher drink prices and smoking bans in many countries and US states, as well as a crackdown on drink driving, meant that many people embraced their ever-increasing selection of drinks at home and took pride in becoming home bartenders and mixologists.

However, being adventurous with booze and fixing cocktails is something many people struggle with. Some fear venturing beyond opening a bottle of beer or popping a Champagne cork at home, which is why I'm here to help you out. You don't have to be a trained professional or have an extensive selection of drinks to fix decent cocktails. Believe me, it's not as hard, as complicated or as time-consuming as you might think.

So, think of this book as being a helping hand, enabling you to create great times at home. I'm hoping that by reading these recipes, fixing the cocktails and enjoying their flavours, you will start a never-ending journey of epic tastes where you learn the confidence to know that you are an unstoppable cocktail legend. I'm throwing a party and there's something for everyone!

COCKTAIL-MAKING BASICS

Making cocktails doesn't have to be hard. Cocktails are fun and celebratory so the process should be too. Because the experience is so theatrical when you go to a cocktail bar, coupled with the fact that they can often take so long to make it to the table, there is a tendency to think 'I couldn't do this at home' – but that's not true. You can do it! So, here are some tips to remember when making cocktails that will help you feel at ease with the whole process.

PARTS

To make cocktail-fixing easy, it's often handy to work in 'parts' rather than actual measurements. It's all about the ratio of each ingredient for the perfect balance of flavour and texture.

◇ 1 part + 1 part + 1 part means that you have three ingredients of equal measure.

◇ 2 parts of an ingredient means that you have twice as much of that ingredient compared to the others. (It's a bit like doing fractions at school, but with a more interesting result!)

It basically means that as long as you know how much ingredient you have in relation to the other ingredients, it's easy.

If you don't know how much volume is in your drinks measure, or if you don't have one at all, don't worry – as long as you use the correct ratio of ingredients, you'll have a delicious cocktail. No measure? No problem: use a thimble, a shot glass, a ramekin or anything you can find really. As long as they're clean, you're good to go!

And remember, when you make these cocktails, you may have a little more drink than you can fit in the glass, as different brands of glass have different volumes. But never fear – you need to taste as you go and adjust as you see fit. And if there's a splash too much, that's the Bartender's Bonus!

There are times that I don't use parts in cocktail recipes. That's when I'm using a whole bottle of wine (sparkling or otherwise) because it's just easier to use actual amounts. Working out parts when the main ingredient is finite seems like too much hassle! You just have to measure the other parts to fit the puzzle.

PALATES

While we're on the subject of making the perfect cocktail, just remember, everybody's palate is different, so if you want to add more of certain ingredients to your cocktail to make it work for you – do it. There's no right or wrong! Always remember that you can tinker with recipes and amounts as much as you like – it's a question of individual taste and enjoyment.

Also, don't forget that the ingredients that you use in your cocktails may be different to the ones I have at home. There are countless brands of the same drink across the world, and sometimes they taste very different to each other. Even pieces of the same fruit variety vary in flavour. The most important thing is to remember to taste before you serve. After all, that's what the cap on the top of a Boston shaker is made for. Use your own judgement when fixing and serving your cocktails.

EGG WHITES

Egg whites are a great cocktail ingredient. Rather than adding flavour, they add a luxurious and slightly frothy texture. It may sound odd, but they work a treat. When using egg white, it's best to use a medium-sized egg, and shake the ingredients in the shaker for ten seconds before adding the ice. This lets the protein in the egg white begin to form foam with the other liquids, rather than being diluted by the ice. This is known as the 'dry shake'. Before adding ice, carefully take the lid off, as shaking the egg white can create pressure inside the shaker, and shake for a further 20 seconds or so.

To separate the yolk from the white of an egg, hold the egg over a bowl and crack it with a sharp tap by using the back of a knife or on the side of a bowl. Tip the yolk from one half of the eggshell to the other, letting the white run into the bowl as you do so.

If you don't want to use egg whites, use the water from a can of chickpeas (garbanzos), otherwise known as aquafaba. By using a couple of dessertspoons of it in your cocktail shaker, it will give you the same effect.

THE 20-SECOND SHAKE

When using a cocktail shaker with ice, you should shake for at least 20 seconds, which is the amount of time it will take to chill your drink. Feel free to shake it for longer if you'd like it ice cold. My rule is: If your hands start to hurt from clutching the cold shaker, your drink is probably ready!

LOW AND NO ALCOHOL DRINKS

My cocktail recipes do contain alcohol, but if you're not in the mood for the hard stuff, you can replace alcoholic spirits with 'low and no' alcohol alternatives. There are so many good examples out there now, made by reputable producers all over the world. From bourbon and gin to vodka, rum and Tequila, there are loads of them and they come alive when teamed with a complementary mixer.

If you fancy a little kick in your cocktail but you don't want alcohol or don't have any low-alcohol options, some cocktails will work by simply adding a homemade alternative.

◊   Replace clear spirits with a shot of water with a squeeze of lemon or lime juice, which will give the drink a spirit-like kick.

◊   Replace darker spirits with a shot of water with a few dashes of Angostura bitters.

But to be honest, if a cocktail recipe has multiple alcoholic elements and you don't have the correct ingredients, you're probably better off having a tonic water or a juice!

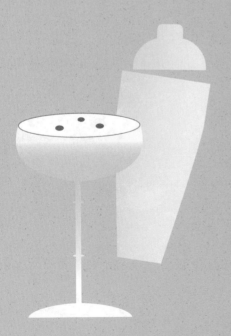

ICE, ICE BABY

There is a misconception around ice in drinks. Some people believe that the more ice you put in, the more it will water down the drink. This isn't true – it's quite the opposite, in fact. Putting only a couple of cubes of ice in your drink means that the ice warms up quicker than if there was lots of ice in it. This results in your drink being diluted faster. Fill a glass with ice and the drink will stay cooler for longer, and so will the ice! The more ice the better. As a general rule of thumb, a handful of ice cubes is enough for a cocktail shaker or a small jug but be a bit more generous for a large jug or pitcher, and fill glasses with ice – but, as always, it's your choice.

And what shape ice should you use? Ice tends to come in two basic forms: cubed and crushed. It's up to you which you use but I would put cubed ice in a cocktail shaker and in a jug or pitcher to chill the ingredients before they get to the glass and in many cocktails that I serve. Crushed ice is lovely in some cocktails that warrant being diluted quicker (as smaller ice melts faster than larger ice). But my curveball ice suggestion is literally a ball! The large spherical ice cube has gained in popularity and adds a touch of theatre to your drink. Moulds are widely available. OK, it's not for everyone, but if you're using a lowball glass, give it a go for a bit of variety.

TO MUDDLE OR NOT TO MUDDLE

Muddling is the technique sometimes used to release flavours and aromas from herbs and fruit. It's a great way of getting the most out of your ingredients. It's easy as pie to do, so don't be afraid to give it a go.

◊   First, drop your herb and/or cut fruit into your cocktail shaker, jug, pitcher or glass.

◊   Then find a muddler. You can buy a specific muddler or you can use any clean, long implement – preferably something wooden with a round bottom (see page 10).

◊   Add sugar syrup and whatever spirit you are using then slowly and firmly press the muddler into your receptacle and gently twist it in one direction in order to crush your herbs and/or fruit. (Some people like to muddle with sugar and water separately but I use syrup as it's easier.)

GARNISHES

Garnishes are exciting! I know it's sometimes easy to think, 'oh, why should I bother?' but it will be like the cherry on top of the cake after your expert cocktail antics. It certainly makes your drinks more Instagrammable! Here are some easy tips.

◊ Bash your herbs to make the fragrance come out and work with your cocktail.

◊ A shaving of citrus zest works really nicely on many cocktails. You can create this by taking a vegetable peeler to your fruit or by cutting a piece with a sharp knife. Twist and bend your zest close to the the surface of the drink in order to release the oils, which give fragrance and flavour.

◊ To make a wheel of lime or lemon, simply cut a thin slice of fruit crossways and cut from the edge to the centre so you can sit it on the rim of the glass, or some people just float the slice upright in the glass.

◊ Keep a stash of re-useable or biodegradable accessories to hand in case of emergency cocktail fixing. Having cocktail sticks (toothpicks), straws and cocktail umbrellas can make all the difference.

SIP HAPPY

Cocktail drinking should be celebratory – they are a symbol of good times. This book is more than just a cocktail recipe book, it's a book that encourages happiness. I am keen to engage my enthusiastic palate to give you drink suggestions for sipping with a massive smile on your face.

In short, I want to encourage people to 'sip happy'. Don't drink to numb the pain, to forget or to get depressed. Drink to celebrate life. Let's focus on the positives and enjoy ourselves. With a cocktail in your hand, there's a lot to smile about!

COCKTAIL-MAKING KIT

There's something pleasing about accumulating your own collection of cocktail equipment. The glint of light as the sun hits the cocktail shaker, the promise of condensation on the ice bucket when you glance at it. It's often when you're doing other things around the house that you see the cocktail equipment and it brings a smile because you know that sometime soon, it'll be cocktail time!

But please don't feel that you have to splash out on specialist equipment in order to enjoy cocktails at home. Here is a guide to some equipment that will help you enjoy the cocktail experience, and some alternatives if you want to go Maverick and do it your own way. In the recipes, I have assumed that you have the basics that you'd find in any kitchen and listed anything a little more unusual so you are not caught out half way through a recipe.

8

JUICER

A lot of citrus fruit are used in cocktail making, so working out what type of juicer you like is essential. Those lemons and limes won't juice themselves and the juice always tastes better when it's freshly squeezed.

Before you start with one of the hand juicers, make sure you have a bowl ready to catch the juice!

THE HAND REAMER

The simplest option, this is a ribbed stick that you hold in your hand, jab the fruit and twist in order to extract the juice. I love this type of juicer.

THE MEXICAN ELBOW SQUEEZER

You'll get a workout for your hands with this one as you squeeze the two handles together in order to extract the juice.

THE CLASSIC JUICER

An easy way to get your hands sticky, this juicer sits on top of a bowl, you impale the fruit on top of the juicing point and rotate to extract the juice. The juice collects in the bowl, catches the pips and it's easy to pour it out. This is probably the easiest way to juice.

THE JUICY SALIF

This is the design icon that looks like it's from *War of the Worlds*. It's surely the sexiest piece of equipment you will ever use at your home bar. Just make sure you put a bowl underneath in order to collect the juice.

ELECTRIC JUICERS

These come in many forms, but essentially, they take the wrist action out of juicing if you feel life's too short to juice manually.

NO JUICER

If you don't have a juicer, you can slice fruit in two and use a teaspoon to remove the juice by twisting the fruit in one hand with the spoon in the other. Or simply apply pressure to the cut fruit with your hands.

CHOPPING BOARD AND SHARP KNIFE

It's always good to have a chopping board handy, not just for chopping fruit, but also to use as your surface when you're juicing and measuring liquids. It's much easier to wash your chopping board in the sink than mopping up the spillages on your counter top! And if you have space, why not buy a chopping board that you use only for cocktails. If you do that, the occasion of cocktail fixing can feel all the more special.

If you like to fix cocktails, you'll know that there's a lot of fruit slicing involved! You know what a kitchen knife is, right? So you don't need me to do a lot of explaining here and I won't add it to the equipment needed. But I just wanted to make sure that you know to keep your knife as sharp as possible. Over time, your knife will blunt the more it's used. Make sure you sharpen your knife regularly because a sharp knife when used correctly is a safe knife. When it's sharp, you put less physical pressure on the knife because the sharp edge is doing all the work for you. It's much safer using a sharp knife to cut than a blunt one.

MEASURES

For many cocktails it's essential that you have a measure. I love using a jigger – a small, hourglass-shaped bar tool which allows you to measure two different amounts. But if you don't have one, just use a shot glass or a ramekin. It doesn't matter if you don't know how much liquid they hold; as long as you work in parts (see page 4) you will still get the same delicious cocktails.

MUDDLER, PESTLE AND MORTAR

In order to muddle – which simply means crushing herbs and fruit to release their flavours – you need a muddler. You can buy specialist muddlers that have rounded, blunt ends and do the trick but, if you don't have one, using a rolling pin or a wooden spoon works just as well.

Alternatively, that classic duo, the pestle and mortar, are great allies in your quest to muddle your herbs and fruit. They're heavy duty and look impressive. You can get properly hands-on and can effortlessly muddle the ingredients you need for your cocktails.

COCKTAIL SHAKERS

Using a cocktail shaker just makes the whole cocktail-fixing experience feel special. There is something about shaking the ingredients with ice until the shaker condensates, then straining the delicious liquid off the ice into the glass that I just love!

There are two main types of shaker and both have their advantages.

THE COBBLER SHAKER

This is a classic, sexy-looking shaker which was created in the 19th century when a removable cap was added to the classic two-piece French shaker. It's really easy to use, is usually drip free and perfect for fixing a couple of Martinis or drinks bound for a coupe glass (see page 13). It is made up of three parts: the main body, the top and the lid. Once a cocktail is shaken with ice, it can be slightly tricky to open but if you run the shaker under a warm tap, this sorts out the problem. I love that you can use the lid as a little taster to see if the cocktail is up to scratch. It's my favourite shaker to use at home.

THE BOSTON SHAKER

The Boston is a two-piece shaker consisting of a large metal base cup and a Boston glass or metal cup that wedges in the top once you're ready to shake. The advantage of this shaker is that you can fit more in than you can in a Cobbler as it has a greater volume. But the downside is that you have to bash the glass to remove it from the base – and I always worry that I'm going to smash the glass! (But that's just me being cautious!)

WHAT CAN I USE INSTEAD?

If you don't have a shaker, never fear – you can stir many cocktails that you shake so you could make them in a glass jug (pitcher) if you like. It's really up to you whether you'd like to have them shaken or stirred.

If you are using egg white, however, it is best to shake the cocktail, otherwise you won't get the required frothy texture. So, if you need to shake but you don't have a shaker, use a jam jar or a water bottle. It has exactly the same effect as a shaker.

STRAINER

I'll be honest here ... I don't always use a strainer as I quite like my cocktails *au naturelle*. But I know that some cocktails should be free from the fruity bits that get in the shaker after squeezing fruit and a fine-mesh strainer makes sure that you don't get fibrous pieces of fruit or pips in your drinks.

If you don't have a specialised cocktail strainer, strain your juice through a small sieve or tea strainer.

JUGS AND PITCHERS

Glass jugs are great for pre-measuring and serving. I make sure I have various sizes to hand. Sometimes you only need a small one when stirring a small cocktail for two, but at other times I use larger jugs – or pitchers as they're known – to mix and serve. If you're using a whole bottle of wine (for drinks like mulled wine and lemon drop fizz), it's always nice to have stylish pitchers if you can, but, if you don't have any, you can serve from a saucepan or a mixing bowl – no stress. As long as you've made a great cocktail, don't let anyone judge how you serve it!

STIRRER

When stirring drinks in larger jugs or pitchers, you need a stirrer with a long handle. There's nothing worse than using a spoon that's too small and accidentally getting your fingers in the drink! Specialised stirrers can look beautiful; they are often metal or glass and have features like twisted handles and stylish paddles at the end. If you buy a nice one, it will make the event of fixing cocktails feel special. But if you don't have one, never fear, you can use a wooden spoon or a spatula.

GLASS BOTTLES AND SEALABLE CONTAINERS

These are your best friend when making sugar syrups, sorbets or cocktails in advance. When putting out your recycling, if you see a bottle with a sealable lid, save it, wash it and keep it in a safe place because when you get the urge to make a syrup or a cocktail in advance you'll need something to store it in. And I swear by sealable containers with clipable lids as they are really secure when storing sorbet in the freezer.

GLASSWARE

I love the theatre of glassware! The shape of glass you're using can add to the pleasure of sipping a cocktail. Having a variety of glassware adds to the excitement of fixing a drink and encourages you to make a good job of it. It's so enticing to see your glassware ready for action on the shelf. But that said, please don't beat yourself up if you don't have the 'correct' glass. Use anything you can find in your cupboards. I'd rather you enjoyed the drink you want than go without. Never let anyone make you feel bad because you serve a cocktail in a highball instead of a lowball glass! Who cares? You can serve a cocktail in a coffee mug or a jam jar if you want to!

If I suggest a specific glass or mug, but you'd prefer to use something else, just do it. If you're mixing the spirits, you can certainly mix up the glassware. There are so many types of cocktail glass out there, but here are the glasses that I love to use, and I feel work for all the cocktails featured in this book.

CHAMPAGNE COUPE

Probably the prettiest and most elegant of all glassware, the Champagne coupe teases with its curvatious charms. I was always under the impression that the glass was created in the 18th century and was modelled on or inspired by the breast of Marie Antoinette, the last Queen of France before the French Revolution and wife of Louis XVI of France. Whether this story is true or not, it adds to the decadent and cheeky nature of cocktails served in this glass. If you have the chance, have a look in charity shops, thrift stores and antique shops because there are some beautiful examples out there. I have some crystal coupes that are etched with palm leaves and they always make me smile. Make your cocktails unique by finding a glass that no one else has.

CHAMPAGNE FLUTE

This glass is as elegant as the day is long. I love serving fizzy cocktails in Champagne flutes because they remind me of a classic Champagne cocktail. There is also a practical reason that these glasses work so well with sparkling drinks: because of their shape, they only allow a small amount of surface area at the top of the drink, which ensures that the drink does not lose its effervescence. The greater the surface area, the faster the drink will go flat. Although, if I'm honest, I never let a fizzy drink hang around long enough to go flat!

COLLINS

The collins glass is a tall, thin glass tumbler with straight sides, which is slightly thinner

and taller than a highball glass. There's not a huge amount of difference between them but the collins glass looks a little more elegant in my opinion. You don't see them as much as highball glasses, so if you don't have any, or can't get your hands on any, don't worry, just use a highball or even a lowball glass.

HIGHBALL

This is the perfect glass to use when serving cocktails of large volume. Some cocktails contain a lot of liquid ingredients so a highball is great for these. They can also accommodate a large amount of ice. In the absence of a collins glass or a hurricane glass, the highball glass is a great one to have to hand. Oh, and it's also perfect for hydrating yourself with water between cocktails. Believe me – if you can down a highball glass of water in between your cocktails, you'll thank me in the morning!

HURRICANE

Named after the hurricane lamp of the same shape, the curves of this glass say 'party'! It originated in New Orleans, somewhere I certainly associate with cocktails and good times. (Although you won't find a Hand Grenade in this book; I think that's a cocktail you have to have on Bourbon Street!) This shapely glass lends itself to fruity, fun cocktails and is the sort of glass I associate with sunny beaches. So when you fancy that full-on holiday experience at home, whip out your hurricanes!

LOWBALL

Also known as an old-fashioned glass or a rocks glass (because of the fact it's perfect for spirits and cocktails 'on the rocks' – in other words poured over ice), this is my favourite glass for sipping a gin and tonic. There's something satisfying about how a lowball glass feels in your hand. The ones I use at home are heavy-based and have an art deco etch to them. I love that you can also use large ice in them. I mention large spherical ice in a couple of recipes and this is the only glass that can accommodate ice of such girth!

MARTINI GLASS

The martini glass is a classic. This stemmed glass with an inverted cone top is a true stunner. It's essentially a modern take on the Champagne coupe, which came first, and the slightly more rounded cocktail glass of the 19th century. Some believe the martini glass came about as part of the American prohibition movement, but it actually had its formal outing at the 1925 Paris Exhibition and became steadily popular throughout the 20th century. I love the stylish lines and the fact that it gives a cocktail a large surface area so you can take in the fragrance of the drink. They are great for flavoursome, strong cocktails that you sip in small amounts.

METAL MUG WITH HANDLE

Although they're not made of glass, I wanted to include this receptacle here. There are a few occasions where you need a metal mug with a handle. Some cold cocktails traditionally come in them for one reason or another, but it's when serving warm cocktails that they come into their own. If sipping a drink like mulled wine or a hot toddy, you don't want to be clutching a hot glass with no handle. There's always the risk that if the drink is too hot, you don't just risk scalding yourself but you risk shattering the glass if it's not heatproof. Copper or brass mugs are a lovely addition to your cocktail bar but if you can't find any, you can just serve warm cocktails in a mug or teacup.

STEMMED DESSERT WINE GLASS

Dessert wine is sweeter than dry white and red and therefore you don't drink as much of it. The stemmed dessert wine glass is an elegant little glass which I use all the time for many sweeter or richer drinks that you enjoy in small sips: sherry, Irish cream, sweet liqueur and so on. These little glasses come with a variety of bowl shapes and all are perfect for rich, sweet drinks like Cauldron Eggnog (see page 100), Irish Coffee Stout Shake (see page 104) and Bananaruma (see page 92).

STEMMED WINE GLASS

There's something a bit naughty about putting a cocktail in a wine glass, not least because purists would say you should only put wine in one. However, a wine glass filled with a delicious cocktail can be fun. The shape of the glass gives instant promise to the drink. If you don't have specific cocktail glassware, always feel you can rely on a stemmed wine glass for support. And it's a great glass to serve cocktails that actually contain wine!

15

SIMPLE SYRUPS

These flavoured syrup recipes will allow you to create cocktails with just the right level of sweetness – plus they make cocktails really fun. They're also great to add to tonic and fizzy waters if you fancy a non-alcoholic tipple, and are brilliant to use in order to pep up a drink that feels a little lacklustre.

Each of these syrup recipes will make more than you need for a cocktail or two, so you can store them in the fridge once they've cooled down and you can enjoy them whenever you need them.

Always use a sterilised bottle or airtight container to store your syrups. To sterilise, simply put them through a hot wash in the dishwasher (or wash by hand), then submerge in boiling water and drain off the water. Let them dry completely before filling.

Note that if you are using commercial syrups, the sweetness and strength of flavour may be different to the recipes here, so use bought syrups sparingly and adjust quantities to taste.

SIMPLE SUGAR SYRUP

MAKES ABOUT
250ML/8FL OZ

I use this basic syrup in lots of cocktails, so it's a good idea to keep a bottle in the fridge because, if you like fixing cocktails, you'll use it more often than you think.

EQUIPMENT

- saucepan
- wooden spoon
- sterilised airtight container

INGREDIENTS

200g/7oz caster (superfine) sugar

100ml/4fl oz water

METHOD

① Put the sugar and water into a saucepan and heat gently, stirring occasionally, until the sugar has dissolved.

② Bring to the boil, then reduce the heat and stir.

③ Once the sugar has dissolved, remove from the heat and leave to cool, then pour into a container. This will last in the fridge for up to 3 weeks.

SMOKY SYRUP

MAKES ABOUT
250ML/8FL OZ

This syrup is a game-changer! If you like the rich, smoky flavour of whiskey and bourbon, this makes a uniquely beguiling accompaniment – you just have to try it in my Smoky Whiskey Sour (see page 58).

EQUIPMENT

- saucepan
- wooden spoon
- sterilised airtight container

INGREDIENTS

200ml/7fl oz honey

50ml/2fl oz water

1 tsp smoked paprika

1 tsp dried chilli flakes

METHOD

① Put the honey and water into a saucepan and heat gently, stirring occasionally, until the honey has dissolved.

② Bring to the boil, then reduce the heat, add the smoked paprika and chilli flakes, stir and simmer for 10 minutes.

③ Remove from the heat and leave to cool. Pour into a container and leave to infuse for an hour (if you can leave it for 24 hours, even better). This will last in the fridge for up to 3 weeks.

CITRUS SYRUP

MAKES ABOUT 350ML/12FL OZ

The zing of citrus can be such a welcome addition to a cocktail. This syrup sums up the excitement of real lemon and lime flavours in one beautiful liquid, and raises the taste profile of the cocktails it is used in like you wouldn't believe.

EQUIPMENT

- sterilised airtight container
- vegetable peeler
- saucepan
- wooden spoon
- juicer
- fine-mesh strainer

INGREDIENTS

2 lemons

2 limes

180g/6¼oz caster (superfine) sugar

160ml/5½fl oz water

METHOD

① Using a vegetable peeler, take the zest off the lemons and limes, making sure that you don't take off the white pith underneath (as this will make your syrup bitter).

② Put the zest into a saucepan with the sugar and water and heat gently, stirring occasionally, until the sugar has dissolved.

③ Bring to the boil, then reduce the heat and simmer for 5 minutes. Remove from the heat.

④ Meanwhile, halve and juice the lemons and limes. Pour the juice into the pan through a fine-mesh strainer so that you can separate pips and fibre from the juice.

⑤ Let the syrup cool, then remove the zest. Pour the syrup into a container and use in your gorgeous cocktails. This will last in the fridge for up to 3 weeks.

GINGER SYRUP

MAKES ABOUT
200ML/7FL OZ

The heat and flavour of ginger is incredible in cocktails. This syrup concentrates the zing and the bite of ginger and makes an incredible addition to your army of cocktail ingredients. It's also great in coffee or hot chocolate.

EQUIPMENT

- vegetable peeler
- saucepan
- wooden spoon
- sterilised airtight container

INGREDIENTS

150g/5oz peeled ginger root

150g/5oz caster (superfine) sugar

200ml/7fl oz water

METHOD

① Cut the peeled ginger into small pieces (5mm/¼in cubes works well).

② Put the sugar and water into a saucepan, add the ginger and heat gently, stirring occasionally, until the sugar has dissolved.

③ Bring to the boil, then reduce the heat and simmer for 30 minutes.

④ Remove from the heat and leave to cool. Remove the ginger and pour the syrup into a container and use in your fabulous cocktails. This will last in the fridge for up to 3 weeks.

COFFEE SYRUP

MAKES ABOUT 300ML/10FL OZ

This syrup is basically a strong, sweet cup of coffee! So whether you like instant coffee, filter coffee, coffee from a cafetière, or coffee from a home pod or bean-to-cup machine, make it however you like. As well as being a great addition to some cocktails, it's lovely in hot milk too.

EQUIPMENT

- kettle or coffee maker
- saucepan
- wooden spoon
- sterilised airtight container

INGREDIENTS

250ml/8fl oz strong coffee

150g/5oz Demerara or muscovado (light brown) sugar

½ tsp vanilla extract (or a small scraping from a split, dried vanilla pod (bean))

METHOD

① Using whatever device you like, make what you consider to be a strong coffee and pour it into a measuring jug. If you are making filter coffee or using a cafetière, use 2 heaped tablespoons of coffee per 250ml/8fl oz of water. If you are using a pod machine or bean-to-cup machine, you will have to use your own discretion where strength and flavour are concerned.

② Put the coffee and sugar into a saucepan and heat gently, stirring occasionally, until the sugar has dissolved.

③ Bring to the boil, then reduce the heat and simmer for 1 minute.

④ Remove from the heat and leave to cool. Once cool, pour the syrup into a container and use in your fabulous cocktails. This will last in the fridge for up to 3 weeks.

BERRY SYRUP

MAKES ABOUT
300ML/10FL OZ

If you like berry sweetness, this recipe is for you. You can use fresh fruit or bags of frozen berries. I adore the flavour that this syrup gives. It's not just great in cocktails but it's amazing diluted with sparkling water and served over ice. You can use whatever berries you like, but I tend to find that red berries are the best, particularly raspberries. A 70/30 split of raspberries and strawberries also works a treat.

EQUIPMENT

- saucepan
- wooden spoon
- masher
- muslin (cheesecloth) or a fine-mesh strainer
- sterilised airtight container

INGREDIENTS

150g/5oz caster (superfine) sugar

200ml/7fl oz water

300g/10oz mixed berries (or whatever berries you desire)

METHOD

① Put the sugar and water into a saucepan and heat gently, stirring occasionally, until the sugar has dissolved. Add the berries.

② Bring to the boil, then reduce the heat and simmer for 25 minutes. As it simmers, mash the berries with either a masher, a spatula, a large spoon or a large fork. Be sure to stir the mixture every 10 minutes or so to make sure it is not sticking to the bottom of the pan. Also, make sure you don't allow the mixture to boil over. The berries have a tendency to froth up in the pan.

③ Remove from the heat and leave to cool.

④ Strain the mixture through muslin or a fine-mesh strainer, being sure to press the fruit pulp with a large spoon or spatula so you can extract as much liquid as possible. Pour into a container and use in your delicious cocktails. This will last in the fridge for up to 3 weeks.

CLASSICS

Sometimes, only a classic cocktail will do. There are so many new creations these days that it can be hard to know what to drink. But if in doubt, start with a classic. There's something beguiling about delving into the collective history of cocktails and sipping something that is time-honoured. But even classics don't have just one recipe or serving suggestion. The cocktails here are some of my favourite easy-to-make classics, the way I like to serve them.

CLASSIC STRAIGHT-UP PARTY MARGARITA

MAKES 2 SERVINGS

My favourite cocktail is a Margarita. I love the mix of Tequila, triple sec and lime juice, as well as the salty rim. It will always be my go-to cocktail wherever I am in the world at any time of year. I produced a series with chef James Martin in the USA. We travelled from coast to coast and I always loved a Margarita after a long day's filming. The drink can be served shaken with ice (on the rocks), blended with ice (frozen) or without ice (straight up) – which is how I like to serve it. It's a great example of how easy a cocktail is to make.

I have suggested you use Reposado Tequila, which is aged in oak for at least two months to give the drink a smooth smokiness, but it doesn't matter if you can't get it. Just use silver or white Tequila if necessary.

I love my Margaritas really zingy, so I don't add sugar or agave syrup, but some recipes do. If you fancy a dash of sweetness, make the cocktail, taste it and add a couple of teaspoons of syrup.

PROPORTIONS

2 parts Tequila

1 part lime juice

1 part triple sec

INGREDIENTS

150ml/5fl oz Tequila Reposado

75ml/2½fl oz fresh lime juice

75ml/2½fl oz triple sec

handful of ice cubes

TO GARNISH

sea salt flakes (for the rim)

2 shavings of lime zest

EQUIPMENT

- 2 martini glasses
- small plate
- juicer
- cocktail shaker
- fine-mesh strainer

METHOD

① Rub a little of the Tequila around the rim of the glasses (use a clean finger). Sprinkle the salt on a small plate and upturn the glasses on the plate so the salt sticks to the rim. Stand the glasses upright.

② Put the liquid ingredients into a cocktail shaker with a handful of ice cubes and shake for about 20 seconds until the shaker is extremely cold to the touch. Strain into the glasses.

③ To garnish, cut two thin shavings of lime zest, twist to release the oils, then add one to each glass.

NEGRONI

MAKES 2 SERVINGS

The Negroni is a popular Italian cocktail made of equal parts gin, vermouth rosso (semi-sweet or sweet red vermouth) and an amaro like Campari, garnished with orange zest. It is considered an apéritif. Traditionally it's stirred not shaken, to avoid froth.

Controversially, you could add a little tonic or soda water to make a longer version if you find the cocktail a little strong – as there is no non-alcoholic mixer in this cocktail.

INGREDIENTS

75ml/2½fl oz gin

75ml/2½fl oz sweet red vermouth

75ml/2½fl oz Campari

2 large spheres of ice (or just a few large ice cubes will do)

TO GARNISH

2 shavings of orange zest

PROPORTIONS

1 part gin

1 part sweet red vermouth

1 part Campari

METHOD

① Put the liquid ingredients into a jug and stir gently.

② Add ice to the 2 glasses, then pour in the cocktail mix.

③ To garnish, cut two thin shavings of orange zest, twist to release the oils, then add one to each glass.

EQUIPMENT

•   glass jug or pitcher
•   stirrer
•   2 lowball glasses

ESPRESSO MARTINI

MAKES 2 SERVINGS

This classic coffee cocktail is great at the end of any meal – perfect if you fancy a coffee but you want to stick to cocktails! It's a lovely option to have with petits fours or a box of chocolates too. If you want to try something a bit different, adding a couple of shakes of Tabasco sauce and a sprinkling of chilli flakes can give this cocktail a fiery kick.

PROPORTIONS

2 parts vodka

1 part espresso

1 part coffee liqueur

TO GARNISH

6 coffee beans

INGREDIENTS

150ml/5fl oz vodka

75ml/2½fl oz freshly brewed espresso coffee

75ml/2½fl oz coffee liqueur

2 tsp Simple Sugar Syrup (see page 17) or Coffee Syrup (see page 20) if you want sweet intensity

handful of ice cubes

METHOD

① Put the liquid ingredients except the sugar syrup into a cocktail shaker with a handful of ice cubes and shake for about 20 seconds until the shaker is extremely cold to the touch.

② Taste a little and add some of the sugar syrup if you want it sweeter.

③ Pour into martini glasses and garnish each glass with 3 coffee beans.

EQUIPMENT

- cocktail shaker
- 2 martini glasses

MOSCOW MULE

MAKES 2 SERVINGS

There are conflicting opinions as to where and how the Moscow Mule originated, but it is strongly believed that the cocktail was created in New York by ginger beer and vodka producers who put their heads together while trying to get the public to drink their products. One thing is sure – this refreshing cocktail is a great way to appreciate both beverages. The ginger beer, vodka and lime mix is really invigorating and is a great way to enliven your guest's palates.

PROPORTIONS

2 parts vodka

8 parts ginger beer

1 part lime juice

INGREDIENTS

few handfuls of ice cubes

60ml/2fl oz vodka

240ml/8fl oz ginger beer (the fierier the better!)

30ml/1fl oz fresh lime juice

dash of Angostura bitters

TO GARNISH

2 small sprigs of mint

2 wedges of lime

METHOD

① Fill the copper mugs with ice cubes.

② Put the vodka, ginger beer and lime juice in a jug along with some more ice and stir gently. Pour into the mugs. Add a dash of Angostura bitters to each each cocktail and garnish with a sprig of mint and a lime wedge.

EQUIPMENT

- 2 copper mugs
- glass jug or pitcher
- stirrer
- juicer
- fine-mesh strainer

BLOODY MARY

MAKES 2 SERVINGS

I love a savoury cocktail! The rich flavour of tomato juice here is totally mouth-watering. A Bloody Mary makes the perfect accompaniment to any meal – brunch, lunch and even dinner. It's also a fabulous accompaniment to savoury nibbles before dinner, plus it also tastes great the next morning! If you fancy a Virgin Mary, simply omit the vodka or replace it with water and an extra squeeze of lemon. Instead of using celery, I like to use a carrot baton to stir the drink, but feel free to do what you like.

PROPORTIONS

4 parts tomato juice

1 part vodka

INGREDIENTS

100ml/4fl oz vodka

50g/2oz onion salt

2 generous squeezes of fresh lemon juice

400ml/14fl oz tomato juice

5 dashes of Worcestershire sauce

2 dashes of Tabasco sauce

few handfuls of ice cubes

TO GARNISH

2 thin carrots or long carrot batons (to be used as stirrers)

EQUIPMENT

- 2 highball glasses
- fine-mesh strainer
- small plate
- jug
- juicer

METHOD

① Rub a little of the vodka around the rim of the glasses with a clean finger. Sprinkle the onion salt on a small plate and upturn the glasses on the plate so the onion salt sticks to the rim. Stand the glasses upright.

② Add the liquid ingredients and sauces to a jug with a large handful of ice and stir. (Alternatively, if you have a large shaker, add the ice then the liquid ingredients and sauces and shake for about 20 seconds, until the shaker is extremely cold to the touch.)

③ Fill the glasses with ice cubes and strain in the cocktail. Garnish with a carrot baton to stir the drink.

DARK AND STORMY

MAKES 2 SERVINGS

A Dark and Stormy is both refreshing and comforting. It's great to sip when you want to cool down in the summer, and it's a fantastic treat in the winter months thanks to the combination of dark rum, ginger beer and lime juice. I love adding a dash of cola, bitters and a grind of black pepper for extra flavour.

PROPORTIONS

2 parts dark rum

4 parts hot ginger beer

2 parts cola

1 part lime juice

INGREDIENTS

2 handfuls of ice cubes

100ml/4fl oz dark rum

200ml/7fl oz hot ginger beer

100ml/4fl oz cola

50ml/2fl oz fresh lime juice

2 dashes of Angostura bitters

TO GARNISH

2 wedges of lime

2 grinds of black pepper

METHOD

① Fill the highball glasses with ice cubes. Put more ice into the jug, then pour in the liquid ingredients and stir gently. Strain into the glasses.

② Garnish each drink with a wedge of lime and a grind of black pepper.

EQUIPMENT

- 2 highball glasses
- glass jug or pitcher
- stirrer
- fine-mesh strainer
- juicer

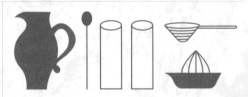

GIMLET

MAKES 2 SERVINGS

It's easy to overlook a Gimlet on a cocktail menu but it is so much more than the sum of its parts. It's hard to believe that a cocktail with only these three ingredients can taste so good. Traditionally it's made with lime cordial but it's really worth making the sugar syrup for the ultimate citrus sensation. However, if you like the traditional flavour of pre-made lime cordial, add a dash for a familiar and traditional sweetness.

PROPORTIONS

4 parts gin

1 part lime juice

1 part Citrus Syrup

INGREDIENTS

handful of ice cubes

160ml/5½fl oz gin

40ml/1½fl oz fresh lime juice

40ml/1½fl oz Citrus Syrup (see page 18)

TO GARNISH

2 wheels of lime

METHOD

① Put the liquid ingredients into a cocktail shaker with a handful of ice cubes and shake for about 20 seconds until the shaker is extremely cold to the touch.

② Strain into the glasses and garnish with a wheel of lime.

EQUIPMENT

* cocktail shaker
* 2 coupe glasses
* fine-mesh strainer
* juicer

MAI TAI

MAKES 2 SERVINGS

When I married my husband, we decided we wanted to honeymoon at a destination that neither of us had been to before. It turned out that, as kids, we'd both wanted to go to Hawaii so off we went. When we got there, we fell in love with the 'Aloha State' and its signature cocktail. So, here's a way to create Hawaiian sunshine from your home drinks bar!

There are so many recipes out there for fixing a Mai Tai. Some use orange juice, some don't, some use pineapple juice, some don't. So, I've used both to create the ultimate beachside sundowner. If you find this delicious fruitiness a bit too sweet, take the juice from half a lemon and squeeze half of it into each drink.

PROPORTIONS

2 parts white rum

1 part dark rum

1 part triple sec

1 part lime juice

1 part almond syrup

1 part pineapple juice

1 part orange juice

INGREDIENTS

2 handfuls of ice cubes

100ml/4fl oz white rum

50ml/2fl oz dark rum

50ml/2fl oz triple sec

50ml/2fl oz fresh lime juice

50ml/2fl oz almond syrup

50ml/2fl oz fresh pineapple juice

50ml/2fl oz fresh orange juice

EQUIPMENT

- 2 lowball glasses
- juicer
- cocktail shaker
- fine-mesh strainer

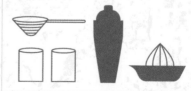

TO GARNISH

2 wedges of lime

2 sprigs of mint

few dashes of Angostura bitters
(optional)

METHOD

① Fill the lowball glasses with ice cubes.

② Put all liquid ingredients into a
shaker with a handful of ice and shake
for 20 seconds.

③ Fill the glasses with ice, strain the
contents of the shaker into the glasses
and decorate with the lime and mint.
Add a dash or two of Angostura bitters
if desired.

MOJITO

MAKES 2 SERVINGS

One of the first cocktails I ever tasted as a late teen, the Mojito certainly whetted my appetite for cocktail discovery. The kick of the rum along with the zing of the sweet lime and mint combination is magical. I love the way that this Cuban classic makes me think of summer all year round.

If you want to give your mojito an edge, try adding a few basil leaves into the muddling process. This will make it super herbaceous.

PROPORTIONS

1 part Simple Sugar Syrup

2 parts white rum

2 parts sparkling water

INGREDIENTS

4 limes

handful of fresh mint leaves (about 40 leaves)

100ml/4fl oz Simple Sugar Syrup (see page 17)

2 handfuls of crushed ice (if you don't have crushed ice, just use small ice cubes)

200ml/8fl oz white rum

200ml/8fl oz sparkling water (or just fill to the top)

TO GARNISH

sprigs of mint

EQUIPMENT

- small glass jug
- muddler
- 2 collins glasses

METHOD

① Cut the limes into eighths. Set two pieces aside for the garnish.

② Place the remaining lime, mint leaves and the sugar syrup into a small jug. Muddle these ingredients together until the mint is ripped up and the lime juice has been released. (To muddle, see page 6.)

③ Pour the rum into the glasses. Use a spoon to share the contents of the jug evenly between the glasses, leaving the lime pieces in the jug. Gently fill the glass with the crushed ice and top up with sparkling water to taste.

④ Stir and garnish by putting the remaining 2 lime wedges in each glass and topping with a sprig of mint.

MANHATTAN

MAKES 2 SERVINGS

A Manhattan, in my opinion, is a more interesting twist on an Old Fashioned. (An Old Fashioned uses sugar instead of vermouth as a sweetener.) I love that the Manhattan cocktail conjures up images of busy cocktail bars in New York City. And I get curious about what Manhattan would have looked like when this cocktail was created in the 1880s. I also adore sweet red vermouth as an ingredient. It adds an element of sophistication to this cocktail. So if you're looking for a strong yet classy sip, she's your gal! You could even try adding a teaspoon of maple syrup for a richer sweetness.

PROPORTIONS

2 parts bourbon

1 part sweet red vermouth

INGREDIENTS

few handfuls of ice cubes

200ml/7fl oz bourbon

100ml/4fl oz sweet red vermouth

3 dashes of Angostura bitters

TO GARNISH

2 shavings of orange zest

2 maraschino cherries

METHOD

① Fill the lowball glasses with ice cubes.

② Put a handful of ice cubes into a small jug. Put all the ingredients into the jug and stir gently. Pour into the glasses.

③ To garnish, cut two thin shavings of orange zest, twist to release the oils, then add one to each glass with a maraschino cherry.

EQUIPMENT

- small glass jug
- stirrer
- 2 lowball glasses

LONG ISLAND ICE TEA

MAKES 2 SERVINGS

There's something completely invigorating about this wonderful cocktail. OK, it has the refreshing look of an actual iced tea, but boy does it pack a punch! Some people add a dash of sweetness by using a teaspoon of Simple Sugar Syrup (see page 17), but for me, there's no need, as the flavour combo of five spirits, lemon juice and cola really hits the spot!

PROPORTIONS

1 part Tequila Reposado

1 part vodka

1 part white rum

1 part triple sec

1 part gin

1 part lemon juice

4 parts cola

TO GARNISH

2 wheels of lemon

INGREDIENTS

2 handfuls of ice cubes

50ml/2fl oz Tequila Reposado

50ml/2fl oz vodka

50ml/2fl oz white rum

50ml/2fl oz triple sec

50ml/2fl oz gin

50ml/2fl oz fresh lemon juice

200ml/8fl oz cola (or just fill to the top)

METHOD

① Put a handful of ice cubes in a large jug, then add the alcoholic liquids and lemon juice and stir gently.

② Fill the glasses with ice and divide the cocktail between them. Top up with the cola.

③ Garnish by adding a lemon wheel to each of the cocktails.

EQUIPMENT

- large glass jug or pitcher
- juicer
- stirrer
- 2 highball glasses
- fine-mesh strainer

SIDECAR

MAKES 2 SERVINGS

The exact origin of the Sidecar is unclear, but some believe it was first created around the end of the Second World War. The Ritz Hotel in Paris claims origin of the drink, which was named after the motorcycle attachment that was very commonly used back then. However, I wouldn't suggest driving after having one of these! If it's a bit too zingy for you, add a teaspoon of Simple Sugar Syrup (see page 17).

PROPORTIONS

2 parts Cognac

1 part lemon juice

1 part triple sec

INGREDIENTS

150ml/5fl oz Cognac

75ml/2½fl oz fresh lemon juice

75ml/23½fl oz triple sec

dash of Angostura bitters

handful of ice cubes

TO GARNISH

2 shavings of lemon zest

METHOD

① Put the liquid ingredients into a cocktail shaker with the ice cubes and shake for about 20 seconds until the shaker is extremely cold to the touch.

② Strain into the glasses.

③ To garnish, cut two thin shavings of lemon zest, twist to release the oils, then add one to each glass.

EQUIPMENT

- cocktail shaker
- 2 Champagne coupes
- fine-mesh strainer
- juicer

PISCO SOUR

MAKES 2 SERVINGS

I fell in love with Pisco Sours when I lived in London and I met an inspirational chef called Martin Morales who opened an amazing Peruvian restaurant in Soho called Ceviche. My love of exciting sour flavours was taken to the next level and, for a while, it may have hit the straight-up Margarita off the top spot! I love to sip a Pisco Sour from a Champagne coupe, but sometimes they are served in small tumblers. I say, freestyle this one and go with the flow. Here's my attempt at making them as good as they do in South America – and in Old London Town!

PROPORTIONS

4 parts Pisco

2 parts lime juice

1 part Simple Sugar Syrup

INGREDIENTS

200ml/7fl oz Pisco

100ml/4fl oz fresh lime juice

50ml/2fl oz Simple Sugar Syrup (see page 17)

1 egg white

handful of ice cubes

TO GARNISH

a few drops of Angostura bitters

METHOD

① Put the Pisco, lime juice, sugar syrup and egg white into a cocktail shaker and shake for 10 seconds. Add a handful of ice cubes and shake again for about 20 seconds until the shaker feels extremely cold to the touch.

② Strain into the glasses and add dots of Angostura bitters on the top.

EQUIPMENT

- juicer
- cocktail shaker
- 2 Champagne coupes
- fine-mesh strainer

WHITE LADY

MAKES 6 SERVINGS

The White Lady is a classic cocktail of epic proportions. I was first introduced to this cocktail by good friends in Richmond upon Thames, on the outskirts of London, who made it for me one Sunday night after dinner – well! … I couldn't quite believe it's vibrancy or poke. It's dangerous and cheeky too. A bit like the lady responsible for serving it to our friends, who then shared it with us. So, here's to you, Shirley!

You might be wondering why this serves six. When my friends introduced me to the drink, it was made in a jug so that we could gently sip it all evening. As it's strong and served in dessert wine glasses, the amount you drink is actually pretty small, so by making a jug of it saves you doing the work several times!

PROPORTIONS

2 parts gin

1 part triple sec

1 part lemon juice

INGREDIENTS

few handfuls of ice cubes

300ml/10fl oz gin

150ml/5fl oz triple sec

150ml/5fl oz fresh lemon juice

TO GARNISH

6 shavings of lemon zest

EQUIPMENT

- glass jug or pitcher
- juicer
- stirrer
- 6 dessert wine glasses
- fine-mesh strainer

METHOD

① Put plenty of ice cubes into a jug, add the liquid ingredients and stir gently. Strain into the glasses.

② To garnish, cut six thin shavings of lemon zest, twist to release the oils, then add one to each glass.

ALTERNATIVE

For a luxurious texture, put half of the ingredients in a shaker with an egg white and shake for 10 seconds, adding a dash of Simple Sugar Syrup (see page 17) if you like your cocktails sweeter. Add a handful of ice cubes, then shake for a further 20 seconds until the shaker feels extremely cold to the touch. Pour into the glasses, repeat with the second half of the ingredients and enjoy.

TWISTS

Once you get to know a cocktail, it's inevitable that you start to think about how you might play with the recipe, or even improve it. I'm always hungry to try new ideas and develop different ways of doing things, so as a result of my inquisitive palate, here, you'll find some of my favourite twists on traditional cocktails. I hope it gets you thinking of how you might jazz up some of the classics too!

CLEMENTINE COSMOPOLITAN

MAKES 2 SERVINGS

This is a twist on one of my favourite cocktails, the Cosmopolitan, which reminds me of trips to New York City. By making this, I imagine I'm spending a city break in one of the USA's finest cities. A standard Cosmo is a great drink, but the added magic of clementine juice takes it to the next level. And here's a tip: don't worry about juicing clementines as some supermarkets and farm shops sell freshly squeezed clementine juice and it is divine – it's also great in a Bucks Fizz. But do track it down – it's oodles better than orange juice.

As an extra twist, you can make this with a clementine sugar rim – just moisten the edges of the glasses with the clementine juice then dip them in two tablespoons of caster (superfine) sugar and a grating of clementine zest.

PROPORTIONS

6 parts vodka

3 parts Triple sec

2 parts cranberry juice drink

2 parts clementine juice

2 parts lime juice

INGREDIENTS

150ml/5fl oz vodka

75ml/2½fl oz Triple sec

50ml/2fl oz cranberry juice drink

50ml/2fl oz clementine juice

50ml/2fl oz fresh lime juice

handful of ice cubes

TO GARNISH

2 wheels of clementine

EQUIPMENT

- cocktail shaker
- juicer
- 2 martini glasses
- fine-mesh strainer

METHOD

① Put the liquid ingredients into a cocktail shaker with a handful of ice cubes and shake for about 20 seconds until the shaker is extremely cold to the touch.

② Strain into each glass and garnish with a thin wheel of clementine.

CIDER SANGRIA

MAKES 2 SERVINGS

This take on a Spanish classic allows us to celebrate our summer holidays from home. I adore the unusual addition of cider which shows how versatile cider is as a cocktail ingredient – even when mixed with red wine. This is great to sip in the sunshine – even in the winter!

To make a batch for a party, use a 750ml/25fl oz bottle of wine and multiply the other amounts by 5.

PROPORTIONS

6 parts red wine

6 parts clementine or orange juice

6 parts cider

2 parts Citrus Syrup

1 part lemon juice

2 parts brandy (optional)

2 parts triple sec (optional)

INGREDIENTS

handful of ice cubes

handful of mixed berries (strawberries and raspberries are lovely here)

1 clementine, sliced

150ml/5fl oz red wine (a fruity Spanish red wine is great)

150ml/5fl oz fresh clementine juice or fresh orange juice (not from concentrate)

150ml/5fl oz cider

25ml/1fl fresh lemon juice

50ml/2fl oz Citrus Syrup (see page 18)

50ml/2fl oz brandy (optional)

50ml/2fl oz triple sec (optional)

METHOD

① Put the ice cubes in the jug with the mixed berries and the sliced clementine. Pour in the red wine, clementine juice, cider, lemon juice, citrus syrup, brandy and triple sec, if using, and stir gently.

② Strain into the glasses, allowing some fruit and ice to drop into each glass.

EQUIPMENT

- large glass jug or pitcher
- juicer
- stirrer
- 2 large tumblers or wine glasses
- fine-mesh strainer

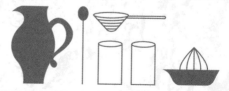

SMOKY WHISKEY SOUR

MAKES 2 SERVINGS

I associate Whiskey Sours with good times. This dates back to having sipped them all evening one night in Dublin, Ireland – but that's a story for another time! A slight tweak to the classic Whiskey Sour can make it even more satisfying to sip and if you like to pair cocktails with food, it's the perfect complement to barbecued offerings, meats especially. By using a smoky aged Scotch or Irish whiskey instead of Bourbon and by adding smoked paprika-infused honey syrup to the cocktail instead of a simple sugar syrup, you can turn a classic cocktail into a twist you'll love.

PROPORTIONS

4 parts whisky/whiskey

2 parts lemon juice

1 part Smoky Syrup

INGREDIENTS

200ml/8fl oz Scotch/Irish whiskey

100ml/4fl oz fresh lemon juice

50ml/2fl oz Smoky Syrup (see page 17)

1 egg white

few handfuls of ice cubes

TO GARNISH

2 cherries

2 slices of orange

METHOD

① Put the liquid ingredients into a cocktail shaker and shake for about 10 seconds. Add a handful of ice cubes and shake for a further 20 seconds until the shaker is extremely cold to the touch.

② Add some more ice cubes to the glasses, then strain the cocktail into them.

③ Thread one cherry and one orange slice on each cocktail stick and add one to each drink to garnish.

EQUIPMENT

- cocktail shaker
- fine-mesh strainer
- 2 lowball glasses
- juicer
- 2 cocktail sticks (toothpicks)

DAIQUIRI BLUSH

MAKES 2 SERVINGS

The Daiquiri is a family of cocktails with the main ingredients being rum, citrus juice and sugar or other sweeteners. There are many variations of Daiquiris on cocktail menus all over the world – you often see strawberry versions in bars but I have my own concoction that is super-exciting and actually pretty invigorating. It uses a berry syrup to give a subtle fruitiness and a gentle pink hue.

PROPORTIONS

3 parts white rum

2 parts lime juice

1 part Berry Syrup

INGREDIENTS

120ml/4fl oz white rum

80ml/2½fl oz fresh lime juice

40ml/1¼fl oz Berry Syrup (see page 21) or grenadine

handful of ice

TO GARNISH

2 wheels of lime

METHOD

① Put the liquid ingredients into a cocktail shaker with the ice cubes and shake for about 20 seconds until the shaker feels extremely cold to the touch.

② Strain into the glasses and garnish with wheels of lime.

EQUIPMENT

• cocktail shaker
• 2 Champagne coupes
• fine-mesh strainer
• juicer

SUPERSONIC AVIATION

MAKES 2 SERVINGS

This cocktail is in celebration of the days of Concorde – a plane my parents had an association with when they worked at Rolls Royce in Bristol, England, in the 1960s and 70s. The Supersonic Aviation contains pale dry vermouth and pomegranate juice, which aren't in a standard aviation cocktail and is a nod to the airplane-based Cinzano adverts of the 1970s and 1980s which starred jet-setting star Joan Collins and British comedian Leonard Rossiter. Cheers to them, cheers to my beautiful parents, and cheers to the legacy of Concorde!

PROPORTIONS

3 parts gin

3 parts white dry vermouth

2 parts maraschino liqueur

1 part crème de violette

3 parts lemon juice

1 part pomegranate juice

INGREDIENTS

75ml/3fl oz gin

75ml/3fl oz dry white vermouth

50ml/2fl oz maraschino liqueur

25ml/1fl oz crème de violette

75ml/2½fl oz fresh lemon juice

handful of ice

25ml/1fl oz pomegranate (or cranberry) juice

TO GARNISH

4 maraschino cherries

METHOD

① Put the liquid ingredients into a cocktail shaker with a handful of ice cubes and shake for about 20 seconds until the shaker is extremely cold to the touch.

② Strain into the glasses and garnish with maraschino cherries threaded onto the cocktial stick.

EQUIPMENT

- cocktail shaker
- 2 martini glasses
- juicer
- fine-mesh strainer
- 2 cocktail sticks (toothpicks)

GIN FIZZ REFRESHER

MAKES 2 SERVINGS

When I want to kick the evening off, sometimes I have a dilemma: do I want gin or do I want a fun fizzy creation? With this drink, that all-important question doesn't need answering – as you have both in one glass. This luxurious and refreshing, gently bubbling drink is just the ticket to get any party started with a smile. The use of maple syrup gives the cocktail real character as well as a welcome hint of sweetness.

I make this with equal parts gin to fizzy water as it has a lovely texture in your mouth along with the frothy egg white, but if you like a pokier cocktail, halve the water. It'll give you a lemony gin kick!

PROPORTIONS

4 parts gin

2 parts lemon juice

1 part maple syrup

4 parts soda water

INGREDIENTS

200ml/7fl oz gin

100ml/4fl oz fresh lemon juice

50ml/2fl oz maple syrup

1 egg white

handful of ice

200ml/7fl oz soda water

TO GARNISH

2 shavings of lemon zest

EQUIPMENT

- juicer
- cocktail shaker
- 2 lowball glasses
- stirrer
- fine-mesh strainer

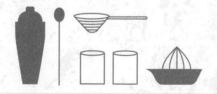

METHOD

① Put the gin, lemon juice, maple syrup and egg white in a cocktail shaker and shake for about 10 seconds. Add a handful of ice cubes and shake for about 20 seconds until the shaker is extremely cold to the touch.

② Strain into the glasses, add the sparkling water to taste and stir gently.

③ To garnish, cut two thin shavings of lemon zest, twist to release the oils, then add one to each glass.

SNOW WHITE RUSSIAN

MAKES 2 SERVINGS

A White Russian is a classically creamy and decadent cocktail. It's delicious at any time of year but I want to give it some extra icy decadence with a scoop of vanilla ice cream. As you make it in the glass, it's an easy one to make just for yourself if you halve the quantities and maintain the proportions. It's also a great alternative to a traditional dessert.

PROPORTIONS

5 parts vodka

3 parts cream

2 parts coffee liqueur

INGREDIENTS

2 scoops of vanilla ice cream

few handfuls of crushed ice (or small ice cubes)

200ml/7fl oz vodka

80ml/2½fl oz coffee liqueur

120ml/4fl oz double (heavy) cream

TO GARNISH

drizzle of coffee liqueur

drizzle of Coffee Syrup (see page 20)

6 candied coffee beans

METHOD

① Take the ice cream out of the freezer and leave for 20 minutes or so to allow it to be properly melty before scooping.

② Put a small amount of crushed ice into each glass (not quite half full). Pour in the vodka, then pour the coffee liqueur around the inner sides of the glass to create a dripping sauce effect. Add the cream and stir briefly to marble the ingredients.

③ Add the ice cream scoops to both glasses.

④ Garnish with a little more coffee liqueur and the coffee syrup and top with the coffee beans.

EQUIPMENT

- 2 lowball glasses
- stirrer
- ice cream scoop

HOT HOT CHOCOLATE

MAKES 2 SERVINGS

Hot chocolate is loved all over the world, and throughout history has taken many forms. This version is a twist on the idea of chilli and chocolate working together in harmony. The recipe is the result of a drunken conversation at a boozy dinner party in Dublin, Ireland. It's both luxurious and daring – and it's so hot, I've told you twice!

If you wanted to add a hint of cinnamon warmth to your hot chocolate, add a pinch to the chocolate when you stir in the cayenne.

PROPORTIONS

4 parts milk

4 parts cream

1 part brandy

INGREDIENTS

200ml/8fl oz whole (full-fat) milk

200ml/8fl oz double (heavy) cream

70g/3oz dark (bittersweet) chocolate, shaved, grated (shredded) or finely chopped

2 generous pinches of cayenne pepper

50ml/2fl oz brandy

TO GARNISH

2 small pinches of cayenne pepper

EQUIPMENT

- saucepan
- whisk
- wooden spoon or spatula
- cups and saucers

METHOD

① Pour the milk and cream into a saucepan, then add the chocolate. Heat gently, whisking constantly, until the mixture simmers and the chocolate has melted. You now have a delicious hot chocolate.

② Add the two generous pinches of cayenne pepper and stir.

③ Allow the mixture to cool slightly for 1 minute or so, then pour in the brandy and stir for a final time.

④ Pour into the teacups with saucers for a decadent touch (use a wooden spoon or spatula to get all the delicious drink from the pan) and add a final pinch of cayenne to garnish.

SHANDYGAFF 21

MAKES 2 SERVINGS

This drink dates back to 19th-century London and was made with two parts lager to one part ginger ale. I've had a play with the recipe and made the drink into something I'd want to sip on a sunny day while waiting for the barbecue coals to heat up. By using ginger beer, you get heat and by adding cider you get crisp bite. It's so refreshing that it whets your appetite for flame-grilled food. This is the 21st-century remix!

And even if you are the designated driver, this is just as delicious when made using low or non-alcoholic lager and cider. There are so many good ones out there these days.

PROPORTIONS

1 part lager

1 part ginger beer

1 part sparkling cider

INGREDIENTS

200ml/7fl oz lager

200ml/7fl oz ginger beer

200ml/7fl oz sparkling cider

few handfuls of ice

TO GARNISH

2 wedges of lemon

METHOD

① Chill all the liquids in the fridge.

② Put a small handful of ice into each glass.

③ Pour the liquid ingredients into a jug, stir gently then pour into the glasses.

④ Let the head settle and squeeze the lemon wedges into the glasses, then use to garnish the cocktails.

EQUIPMENT

- 2 highball glasses
- stirrer
- jug or pitcher

SUMMER AFFOGATO

MAKES 2 SERVINGS

This is where cocktails meet dessert! I love the idea of a traditional affogato – hot espresso over creamy vanilla ice cream – but after a meal, when this is traditionally served, I'm always too full. So, I've created a cocktail that works in a similar way but is much lighter, fruitier and more palate cleansing. I like to make my own sorbet, but if you don't have time, just buy a brand you love.

This is great for kids too. Just warm up some traditional still lemonade and pour over the sorbet instead of the limoncello.

PROPORTIONS

4 parts limoncello to 1 part berry syrup

FOR THE SORBET

500g/1lb 2oz strawberries

100g/4oz caster (superfine) sugar

200ml/7fl oz water

juice of 1 lemon

FOR THE COCKTAIL

200ml/7fl oz limoncello

50ml/2fl oz Berry Syrup (see page 21)

EQUIPMENT

- saucepan
- wooden spoon
- juicer
- freezable container
- ice cream scoop

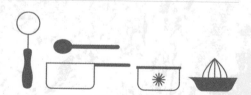

TO MAKE THE SORBET

① Hull the strawberries and halve them if they are large.

② Put the sugar and water into a saucepan and heat gently, stirring occasionally, until the sugar has dissolved. Bring to the boil, then remove from the heat and add the strawberries. Mash the fruit slightly with a potato masher or a large fork, just to break up the strawberries a little. Add the lemon juice, then leave to macerate until cool.

③ Once cool, put the mixture in a blender or food processor and blitz until smooth.

④ Pour the mixture into an ice cream machine and churn until frozen. Or put into a freezable container with a lid and put in the freezer. Stir the mixture once every hour for 4–5 hours until frozen. The sorbet will last in the freezer for up to 2 months.

TO MAKE THE COCKTAIL

① To make the cocktail, take the sorbet out of the freezer and leave for 5 minutes to soften.

② Put the limoncello into a saucepan over a low heat and warm gently. Don't let it boil otherwise you'll get rid of the alcohol and all its punch! Put a scoop of the sorbet into each of the coffee cups, pour the syrup over the sorbet and then the limoncello. Stir with a teaspoon and sip your slushy cocktail.

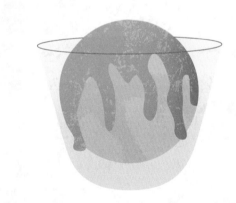

EQUIPMENT

- masher
- food processor or blender
- fine-mesh strainer
- 2 coffee cups and saucers

TEQUILA SUNDOWNER

MAKES 2 SERVINGS

I love the sweet, fruity hit of a Tequila Sunrise, but it's at sunset when I want to drink one, so I've developed the ultimate tropical fruit sundowner with the addition of mango, which complements the orange juice perfectly. If you're not into fruity, sweet cocktails – think again. It's perfect with spicy food like Buffalo wings or chilli squid, because the spice in food like this tempers the sweetness.

If you'd like a longer drink, add a good slug of dry sparkling wine and stir it in, or why not sip this drink without the alcohol. It makes a brilliant breakfast refresher.

PROPORTIONS

2 parts Tequila

4 parts orange and mango juice

1 part Berry Syrup or grenadine

2 parts lime juice

FOR THE MANGO AND ORANGE JUICE

2 mangos

200ml/7fl oz fresh orange juice

FOR THE COCKTAIL

120ml/4fl oz Tequila

240ml/8fl oz mango and orange juice (above)

120ml/4fl oz fresh lime juice

60ml/2fl oz Berry Syrup (see page 21) or grenadine

few handfuls of crushed ice (or small cubes)

TO GARNISH

2 maraschino cherries

2 wheels of orange

EQUIPMENT
- blender or food processor
- glass jug or pitcher
- juicer

METHOD

① To make the mango and orange juice, cube the mango flesh and put it into a blender. Pour in the orange juice and blitz for about a minute, or until smooth.

② Put the ice in a glass jug and pour in the Tequila, the orange and mango juice and the lime juice.

③ Divide the Berry Syrup between the glasses, then half-fill the glasses with crushed ice. Add the Tequila fruit juice mix from the jug.

④ Garnish each glass with a maraschino cherry. Twist the orange wheels onto cocktail umbrellas and stick in a reusable straw so that you can stir the Berry Syrup into the rest of the cocktail.

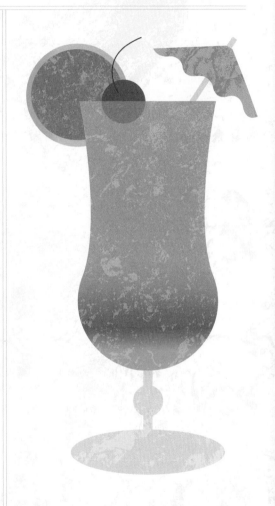

EQUIPMENT

- strainer
- 2 hurricane glasses
- 2 cocktail umbrellas
- 2 reusable straws

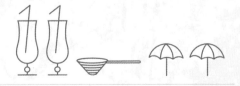

THE ORCHARD DUCHESS

MAKES 6 SERVINGS

I devised this cocktail for Sarah, Duchess of York when we were appearing together on a UK TV programme. I know she loves a tipple and I decided to create a fruity twist on one of my favourite cocktails (the classic Champagne Cocktail) by using one of my favourite fruits: the humble apple! Instead of using Champagne, I use traditional method cider, which is made in a similar way, and instead of brandy, I use Calvados or apple brandy. The sugar lump is replaced by syrup. This cocktail will certainly leave you feeling fruity!

Traditional method cider is sold in a 75cl bottle, just like sparkling wine is (because it is matured in the bottle), so I use the whole bottle here rather than waste it – hence why this serves six.

INGREDIENTS

handful of ice

100ml/4fl oz Calvados or apple brandy

100ml/4fl oz Citrus Syrup (see page 18)

750ml/25fl oz (1 bottle) traditional method dry cider

TO GARNISH

1 apple

METHOD

① Put the ice in a jug or pitcher. Pour the brandy and syrup into the jug, add the cider and stir gently. Pour into the glasses.

② Cut discs of apple, put them on the rim of the glasses and serve.

EQUIPMENT

- glass jug or pitcher
- stirrer
- 6 Champagne flutes or cocktail glasses

BATCH

When preparing for a cocktail party it can be really satisfying to make a batch of cocktails. Rather than using a shaker and only making one or two drinks, you can make multiple cocktails in the same amount of time. Obviously, you can make all the cocktails in this chapter for one or two people, if you like, but they are perfect for a bigger crowd or for making in large batches, stored and served later that day.

In this selection, you'll find some that need a whole bottle of wine and some that are Martini-style drinks, super easy to make in batches.

Many of these can be made ahead of time, but to keep them fresh make them earlier in the day rather than days in advance.

Other batch cocktails in this book include: White Lady (p50), Orchard Duchess (p76), Applevini (p125) and Mulled Wine (p132).

THE MOIRA ROSE

MAKES 6 SERVINGS

I first came up with the idea of this Martini for Mother's Day. I felt it was the perfect celebration for mothers everywhere. And I've decided to name it after one of the strongest fictional mothers of the 21st century: Moira Rose – the classy and unique matriarch of the Rose family in the hilarious Netflix comedy *Schitt's Creek*. Cheers to you and your incredibly captivating family, Moira!

INGREDIENTS

450ml/16fl oz gin

300ml/10fl oz rosé vermouth

150ml/5fl oz pomegranate juice

handful of ice cubes

6 tsp pomegranate seeds

6 sprigs of tarragon

PROPORTIONS

3 parts gin

2 parts rosé vermouth

1 part pomegranate juice

METHOD

① Pour all the liquid ingredients into a jug, stir, cover and leave in the fridge until you need it. If you are making the cocktail to serve immediately, make sure there is a handful of ice cubes in the jug.

② Pour into the glasses and garnish with a spoonful of pomegranate seeds in each glass (which will sink like jewels to the bottom of the glass) and float the sprigs of tarragon on the top.

EQUIPMENT

- large glass jug or pitcher
- stirrer
- 6 martini glasses

FOR 2 COCKTAILS

If you are making this for two people, just reduce the quantities but keep the same proportions.

150ml/5fl oz gin

100 ml/4fl oz rosé vermouth

50ml/2fl oz pomegranate juice

① Put all the liquid ingredients into a cocktail shaker with a handful of ice cubes and shake for about 20 seconds until the shaker feels extremely cold to touch. Pour into glasses and garnish as on previous page.

RASPBERRY FROSÉ

MAKES 6 SERVINGS

The last time I was in Miami, I was relaxing by the outdoor pool one day and the poolside bar opened, talk about good timing! The only thing they served at this bar was frosé – yes, that's frozen rosé. This was the beginning of my love affair with what is basically an alcoholic Slush Puppy (remember them?). Rosé in any form is the perfect partner to sun-drenched days, and my Raspberry Frosé takes it to the next level by celebrating the fruit that epitomises the vibrancy of summer: fresh raspberries. The fruitiness and acidity of this drink also goes really nicely with fruity desserts.

INGREDIENTS

750ml/25fl oz (1 bottle) rosé wine, preferably a pale European rosé

200ml/7fl oz raspberry liqueur

TO GARNISH

handful of berries (I like a mix of raspberries, blueberries, strawberries and blackberries)

METHOD

① Pour the bottle of rosé and the raspberry liqueur into a freezable container that clips shut and leave in the freezer until it has frozen. It is best to leave it overnight or for around 8 hours. Please note that because of the alcohol, it will not freeze totally solid.

② Once it has frozen as much as it can, it will still appear slightly wet in places, making it easy to shatter and stir. Gently jab the frozen mixture with a butter knife. Once it has broken up a bit, stir with a spoon until it is slushy. Spoon it out into the wine glasses and top with the berries.

EQUIPMENT

- freezable container
- spoon
- 6 wine glasses

CHERRY BAKEWELL MARTINI

MAKES 6 SERVINGS

I love cherry Bakewell cakes, and this is the perfect dessert cocktail if you're a cherry and almond lover like me. This is a great cocktail to have when you want something sweet after dinner as it reminds me of my favourite type of afternoon tea cake, without being heavy. I suggest you make a batch ahead of time and serve after dinner – as nobody wants to make a cocktail from scratch after three courses and with a room full of guests!

PROPORTIONS

1 part amaretto

1 part cherry brandy

1 part white vermouth

INGREDIENTS

200ml/7fl oz amaretto

200ml/7fl oz cherry brandy

200ml/7fl oz white vermouth

handful of ice

TO GARNISH

handful of flaked almonds

METHOD

① Pour all the liquid ingredients into a jug, stir, cover and leave in the fridge until you need it. If you are making the cocktail to serve immediately, make sure there is ice in the jug.

② Toast the flaked almonds in a dry frying pan (skillet) over a medium heat, tossing the pan occasionally, until golden brown. Allow them to cool.

③ Once you are ready to serve, pour the chilled cocktail into individual glasses and scatter 3–5 flaked almonds over the top.

EQUIPMENT

- glass jug or pitcher
- stirrer
- 6 martini glasses
- frying pan (skillet)

MINT JULEP

MAKES 6 SERVINGS

This fabulously underrated cocktail, associated with the American South, was originally a medicinal drink which was taken to settle the stomach, but it was in the late 1700s and early 1800s that it became popular as a social drink. The refreshing, punchy nature of this little beauty is a great way to get people's attention at the start of your party, and it's an easy cocktail to prepare in a batch ahead of time.

You can also try making a longer drink by adding a good glug of dry sparkling wine to your mug at the last minute, which is delightfully refreshing.

PROPORTIONS

1 part Simple Sugar Syrup

8 parts bourbon

INGREDIENTS

60 mint leaves (or a large handful)

90ml/3fl oz Simple Sugar Syrup (see page 17)

720ml/24fl oz bourbon

6 handfuls of crushed ice

TO GARNISH

6 small sprigs of mint

6 dashes of Angostura bitters

METHOD

① Put the mint leaves and sugar syrup in a large jug and muddle together. Add the bourbon and stir, cover, then leave in the fridge.

② When ready to serve, fill your mugs with crushed ice and add the mint and bourbon mixture. Garnish with a sprig of mint and a dash of angostura bitters in each mug.

EQUIPMENT

- glass jug or pitcher
- muddler
- 6 copper mugs or julep tims

PUNCHY PEACH TEA

MAKES 6 SERVINGS

Is it a punch? Is it a tea? It's whatever you want it to be. Refreshing on a warm day, this cocktail is fruity and a little bit naughty, and is a great alternative to a hot black tea in the afternoon. I think it's fun to serve it in a teapot with teacups in a nod to Prohibition, but if you don't have a teapot, you could make it in a jug and serve in highball glasses.

PROPORTIONS

5 parts black tea

2 parts peach schnapps

1 part lime juice

INGREDIENTS

500ml/17fl oz black tea (using 3 teabags is easiest)

200ml/7fl oz peach schnapps

100ml/4fl oz fresh lime juice

handful of ice cubes

TO GARNISH

6 sprigs of mint

METHOD

① Boil water in a kettle and pour into a teapot containing the teabags. Stir and leave to brew for 2 minutes. Take out the teabags and leave the tea to cool.

② Once the tea has cooled, add the peach schnapps and lime juice and stir. Chill in the fridge before serving if you have time, but if you don't, put a few cubes of ice in each cup and serve the drink from the teapot. Garnish with sprigs of fresh mint.

EQUIPMENT

- kettle
- large teapot
- stirrer
- juicer
- 6 cups and saucers
- fine-mesh strainer

MANGO MADNESS

MAKES 6 SERVINGS

The mango is a beautiful fruit. It sums up tropical fruity indulgence in its raw form and is simply delicious. But when paired with passionfruit, something exciting happens! So I've created a cocktail that will bring summer sunshine to your door wherever you are in whatever season it happens to be.

To bring even more sweet fruit flavour to your cocktail, you could add 25ml/1fl oz Berry Syrup (see page 21) at the bottom of your glasses before you pour in the drink.

PROPORTIONS

4 parts mango purée

1 part passionfruit purée

1 part lime juice

2 parts white rum

FOR THE MANGO PURÉE

750g/1lb 10oz mango
(about 3 ripe mangos), cubed

150ml/5fl oz water

FOR THE COCKTAIL

handful of ice cubes

600ml/20fl oz mango purée

150ml/5fl oz passionfruit purée
(it's easiest to buy this)

150ml/5fl oz fresh lime juice

300ml/10fl oz white rum

6 handfuls of crushed ice

TO GARNISH

flesh of 2 passionfruit

6 wedges of lime

FOR THE MANGO PURÉE

- blender or food processor
- juicer
- fine-mesh strainer
- airtight container

METHOD

① To make the mango purée, put the cubed mango in a blender with the water and blitz until smooth. Don't rush this! When you think it's done, keep going until it is really smooth.

② Use the back of a spoon to press and rub the pulp through a fine-mesh strainer into an airtight container. Store in the fridge until needed – it will last for up to 3 days – or it will also freeze well.

③ Put the ice cubes in a large jug with the mango purée, the passionfruit purée, lime juice and white rum. Stir until all the ingredients are combined.

④ Fill the glasses with the crushed ice. Pour in the liquid ingredients from the jug, without letting the ice cubes go into the glasses. Garnish each glass with the passionfruit flesh spooned over the top (seeds included if you like the crunch), a lime wedge and add a reusable straw.

FOR THE COCKTAIL

- large glass jug or pitcher
- stirrer
- 6 hurricane glasses
- 6 reusable straws

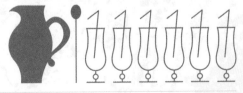

BANANARUMA

MAKES 6 SERVINGS

Named in part after my favourite girl band of all time, Bananarama, I originally developed this recipe imagining it would be a boozy smoothie. When I tasted it with friends, it soon became clear that it is so much better in a small glass, as you'd sip a cream liqueur after dinner. I love the combination of banana and peanut butter and it's even better with spiced rum.

Only add the salt if you are using a low-sodium peanut butter. And even though I love the roasted flavour of peanuts, feel free to use whatever nut butter you like.

Also, using coconut milk is a nice way of making this cocktail dairy free.

INGREDIENTS

2 bananas

300ml/10fl oz whole (full-fat) milk

4 heaped tablespoons peanut butter (crunchy or smooth it's your choice!)

200ml/7fl oz dark spiced rum

pinch of salt (optional)

TO GARNISH

small handful of unsalted roasted peanuts

METHOD

① Peel and chop the bananas and put in a blender. Add the milk, peanut butter, rum and salt, if using, and blend for 1 minute. This will stay fresh for up to 3 days in the fridge.

② When ready to serve, pour into the glasses. Crush the peanuts and sprinkle a small amount over the top.

EQUIPMENT

- blender or food processor
- 6 dessert wine glasses

PEAR ORCHARD WARMER

MAKES 6 SERVINGS

This may look ridiculously simple but it is ridiculously tasty! I have tried to add things to this recipe to make it more fancy, but as it always gets such a positive reaction when I serve it, I thought 'why bother to overthink it?' I love any excuse to socialise outside and this drink is perfect for outdoor gatherings when it's a little cold – a late night barbecue or a bonfire party perhaps. Wherever you decide to try this drink, you won't believe its spicy character is so easy to achieve.

PROPORTIONS

2 parts cloudy pear juice

1 part spiced rum

INGREDIENTS

600ml/20fl oz cloudy pear juice (or apple if you prefer – it's equally delicious!)

300ml/10fl oz spiced rum (or whisky or brandy, if you're a fan)

1 whole nutmeg

TO GARNISH

1 pear, sliced widthways

METHOD

① Put the pear juice into a saucepan and bring to the boil, stirring occasionally. Once it starts to boil, take it off the heat immediately.

② Add the spiced rum and stir. Pour the cocktail into the cups and grate a little nutmeg over the top. Serve with a cross-section slice of pear on the side of each cup.

EQUIPMENT

* saucepan
* wooden spoon
* grater

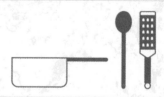

EQUIPMENT

- 6 heatproof cups with handles
  (metal ones are lovely) or just use
  tea cups or coffee mugs

PLUM SAKETINI

MAKES 6 SERVINGS

Plum sake is one of the wonders of Japan. The elegant, ripe fruit flavour of the drink is uniquely divine. Plum and ginger are a combination made in heaven (have you ever added ginger to plums when making a crumble? Well, if you haven't, you should). But if you're not up for making a crumble, promise me you'll fix this cocktail instead. It's my sake-based take on a Martini using decadent ginger syrup and mouth-watering fresh lime juice. It's truly delicious.

PROPORTIONS

4 parts plum sake

1 part Ginger Syrup

1 part lime juice

INGREDIENTS

handful of ice

600ml/20fl oz plum sake

150ml/5fl oz Ginger Syrup (see page 19)

150ml/5fl oz fresh lime juice

TO GARNISH

6 wheels of lime

METHOD

① If making to serve immediately, put the ice cubes in a large jug and add the liquid ingredients. Stir gently until the mixture is cold. Pour immediately into the glasses. Garnish with a wheel of lime on the rim of each glass.

② If making ahead of time, put all liquid ingredients into the jug, but do not add ice. Store in the fridge until ready to serve.

EQUIPMENT

- large jug or pitcher
- juicer
- stirrer
- 6 martini glasses
- fine-mesh strainer

TO MAKE 2 COCKTAILS

It's easy to make this in advance in large quantities, or it can also be made in smaller batches, just maintaining the proportions.

200ml/7fl oz plum sake

50ml/2fl oz Ginger Syrup (see page 19)

50ml/2fl oz fresh lime juice

2 wheels of lime

① You can either stir all the ingredients with ice in a jug or, if you like to use a shaker, put all the liquid ingredients into a cocktail shaker with a handful of ice cubes and shake for about 20 seconds until the shaker is extremely cold to the touch. Pour into the glasses and garnish each one with a wheel of lime on the rim of each glass.

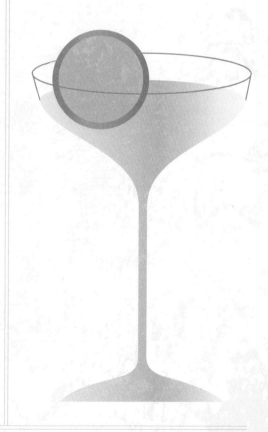

ZESTY HOT TODDY

MAKES 6 SERVINGS

If you're looking for something comforting and restorative but with a racy glint in its eye, you can't go wrong with a hot toddy. But sometimes you might be looking for an extra lick of zing, so I've mixed things up with the zesty heat of triple sec. This will certainly clear out the tubes and re-invigorate the system. It's great for outdoor occasions at night. And if whisky isn't your thing, feel free to try it with bourbon, brandy or spiced rum.

PROPORTIONS

24 parts water

4 parts whisky

3 parts triple sec

1 part clear honey

TO GARNISH

6 wheels of lemon

INGREDIENTS

1.2l/40fl oz water

200ml/7fl oz whisky

150ml/5fl oz triple sec

50ml/2fl oz clear honey

2 cinnamon sticks (broken in half)

4 cloves

3 star anise

juice of 1 lemon

METHOD

① Put the water, whisky, triple sec and honey into a saucepan with the cinnamon stick, cloves and star anise. Heat gently but don't allow it to boil.

② Once heated, add the lemon juice.

③ Divide between your heatproof cups, making sure each one gets some spices. Garnish each cup with a wheel of lemon.

EQUIPMENT

- saucepan
- 6 heatproof cups with handles*
- juicer
- fine-mesh strainer

*glass, brass or copper are great

CAULDRON EGGNOG

MAKES 8 SERVINGS

I've spent years trying to find the perfect Eggnog. It's a drink I love and I associate with winter holidays in the USA. I've never been able to perfect the right recipe, but that doesn't matter because, quite by chance, a good friend of mine introduced me to their version and I simply can't better it! The name is a nod to a restaurant in Bristol, England called The Cauldron, owned by chef Henry Eldon, who devised this recipe. This is a great sweet treat for Halloween evenings as well as Christmas, which the name also suggests!

And yes ... I know that, traditionally, eggnog is sipped in mugs with handles, but because it's so deliciously sweet and rich, I love to sip a small amount in a dessert wine glass.

You will need a thermometer for this one.

INGREDIENTS

1 litre/34fl oz whole (full-fat) milk

5 cloves

2 cinnamon sticks

12 egg yolks

300g/10oz caster (superfine) sugar

1 vanilla pod (bean), split lengthways

1 litre/34fl oz double (heavy) cream

300ml/10fl oz bourbon

1 whole nutmeg

METHOD

① Put the milk into a saucepan with the cloves and cinnamon sticks and bring to the brink of simmering, then remove from the heat.

② In a separate bowl, add the egg yolks and sugar and scrape in the seeds from the vanilla pod. Whisk until light and fluffy. (Obviously, use the whites to make a meringue or a healthy omelette!)

EQUIPMENT

- saucepan
- whisk
- sugar thermometer
- sterilised bottle
- grater

③ Pour the hot milk into the egg mixture, whisking well, then pour it back into the pan and heat gently to 82°C/180°F, stirring constantly. If you don't have a thermometer (although Henry feels you should have one!) don't worry – just make sure you don't let it boil or heat up too quickly. If you do either of these things, or don't stir it enough, the mix will scramble.

④ Remove from the heat, cool, then chill (both you and the drink!)

⑤ While it is chilling, sterilise your bottle by pouring boiling water over the bottle and leaving it to cool and dry.

⑥ Once the egg yolk mixture is chilled, add the cream, bourbon and a good grating of nutmeg. Use a funnel to pour into the sterilised bottle. Chill in the fridge or serve at room temperature.

⑦ To serve, find your favourite dessert wine glasses, shake the bottle to wake the drink, pour, then grate plenty of nutmeg over the top. Now you're ready to sip and enjoy! If you don't finish it all, the drink will last for a week in the fridge.

EQUIPMENT

- 8 dessert wine glasses
  (or glass mugs with handles)

SUMMER SUNSET

MAKES 6 SERVINGS

Nothing says summer like the taste of citrus. And when accompanied by gin, it's the perfect combination to sip as the sun sets. This cocktail requires a dash of sweetness to cut through the citrus zing provided by the grapefruit, lemon and lime, so I've found a way to use up those dusty bottles of sweet dessert wine that you've had lurking at the back of the cupboard. Use them as a characterful sugar syrup in the ultimate sundowner. I need to thank the hugely talented mixologist Eszter Boswell from The Kentish Hare in Kent, England who created a cocktail that I have played with in order to develop this one. Your use of dessert wine as a sweetener is genius!

PROPORTIONS

4 parts gin

4 parts pink grapefruit juice

6 parts Sauternes

1 part citrus juice

INGREDIENTS

18 muddled raspberries

4 large handfuls of ice cubes

300ml/10fl oz gin

300ml/10fl oz pink grapefruit juice

450ml/16fl oz Sauternes (or any pale sweet dessert wine)

75ml/2½ fl oz fresh citrus juice (a mixture of lemon and lime)

6 teaspoons of Berry Syrup (see page 21)

TO GARNISH

6 wheels of pink grapefruit

EQUIPMENT

- pestle and mortar
- fine-mesh strainer
- large glass jug or pitcher
- juicer

METHOD

① Muddle the raspberries (I find this easiest in a pestle and mortar), then strain the pulp through a small fine-mesh strainer and set aside.

② Put a handful of ice cubes into a jug. Add the gin, pink grapefruit juice, lemon and lime juice, Sauternes, raspberry juice and berry syrup and stir gently. If making ahead of time, do not put ice in the jug. Store in the fridge until ready to serve.

③ Fill the glasses with ice cubes, then pour the cocktail into the glasses. Garnish each glass with a wheel of pink grapefruit on the side, to represent the setting sun.

EQUIPMENT

- stirrer
- 6 highball glasses

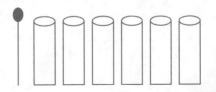

IRISH COFFEE STOUT SHAKE

MAKES 6 SERVINGS

Irish stout is a wonderful ingredient to use when drink-making or cooking. Accompanying it with Irish cream liqueur is a wonderful way to enjoy two of the country's finest offerings. This celebration of Irish drinks is so easy to make and when making it in a batch, it's virtually fuss free. You'll find that the consistency of cream liqueur can vary, so make sure you use a luxuriously thick example; this will give the cocktail the velvety texture required.

If you think that the consistency is a little thin, add a tablespoon of double (heavy) cream. If you'd like a dairy-free version, use a coconut cream-based liqueur.

PROPORTIONS

6 parts Irish stout

3 parts Irish cream liqueur

1 part Coffee Syrup

INGREDIENTS

600ml/20fl oz Irish stout

300ml/10fl oz Irish cream liqueur

100ml/3½fl oz Coffee Syrup (see page 20)

handful of ice cubes

TO GARNISH

6 chocolate-covered coffee beans

METHOD

① Chill all the ingredients.

② Put the liquid ingredients into a jug with a handful of ice and stir gently. Pour into martini glasses.

③ Garnish with the chocolate-covered coffee beans.

④ If making ahead of time, don't put ice in the jug. Once made, cover and store in the fridge until needed.

EQUIPMENT

- glass jug or pitcher
- stirrer
- 6 martini glasses

LEMON DROP FIZZ

MAKES 6 SERVINGS

I love citrus! And lemon gives you that summer feeling whatever time of year it happens to be. I've come across many citrus-based fizzy cocktails, most of which use sugar syrup, but by using my retro hidden gem (a low-priced northern Italian fizz called Asti) you avoid having to make the syrup! The drink is also super simple to make as it contains only three ingredients. And it's one of the best ways to enjoy sparkling wine.

INGREDIENTS

handful of ice cubes

300ml/10fl oz vodka

150ml/5fl oz lemon juice (I don't strain the lemon juice as I love the fleshy bits!)

750ml/25fl oz (1 bottle) Asti or similar sweet sparkling wine

TO GARNISH

sprigs of lemon verbena or lemon balm or just a slice of lemon

METHOD

① Put the ice into a large serving jug. Pour the vodka into the jug and add the lemon juice.

② Open the Asti and gently add to the mix so it doesn't froth up too much! Stir gently, then pour into Champagne flutes.

③ Garnish with sprigs of lemon verbena or lemon balm or, if you can't find any, a sprig of tarragon can be a lovely addition.

EQUIPMENT

* glass jug or pitcher
* juicer
* stirrer
* 6 Champagne flutes

SEASONAL

I like to eat and drink with the seasons. Using seasonal
flavours to keep things interesting year-round is certainly
the way forward. It's easy to keep going back to what you
know and like, but changing it up at different times of the
year makes things fun. I invite you to sip with the seasons,
so here are some loveable ideas to keep cocktail time varied.

COGNAC KICKER

MAKES 2 SERVINGS

Good brandy isn't just for making brandy butter or putting in your cooking, it should be celebrated as the well-crafted and unique drink that it is. Cognac is the really good stuff from western France and is fabulous as a long drink as well as in cocktails. In my opinion, cocktails involving Cognac complement flame-grilled food perfectly – so if you're having the first barbecue of spring, this cocktail will warm and invigorate you in equal measure. If you've never tried Cognac in a cocktail before, give this one a whirl as Cognac marries well with ginger ale and this cocktail is certainly proof of that!

PROPORTIONS

2 parts Cognac

6 parts ginger ale

1 part lime juice

INGREDIENTS

handful of ice cubes

50ml/2fl oz fresh lime juice

100ml/4fl oz Cognac

300ml/10fl oz ginger ale

dash of Angostura bitters

TO GARNISH

2 wedges of lime

METHOD

① Fill the glasses with ice cubes. Pour the lime juice into a jug. Add the Cognac and ginger ale and stir gently. Add a dash of Angostura bitters.

② Strain into the glasses and garnish with a wedge of lime.

EQUIPMENT

- 2 highball glasses
- glass jug or pitcher
- stirrer
- juicer
- fine-mesh strainer

TWINKLE TOES

MAKES 2 SERVINGS

I love to go out in the fun-filled West End of London, dance and drink cocktails until the early hours. The Twinkle is a cocktail I associate with good times at The Ivy where I first tried it. There are many variations but all include dry sparkling wine and some sort of elderflower element – a taste of which is great in late spring, when elderflowers start to blossom. I have my own twist with zingy lemon, which makes a wonderfully flirtatious cocktail to accompany your dancing feet.

PROPORTIONS

1 part vodka

2 parts elderflower liqueur

1 part lemon juice

6 parts dry sparkling wine

INGREDIENTS

25ml/1fl oz vodka

50ml/2fl oz elderflower liqueur

25ml/1fl oz fresh lemon juice

handful of ice cubes

150ml/5fl oz dry sparkling wine

TO GARNISH

shavings of lemon zest

METHOD

① Put the vodka, elderflower liqueur and lemon juice into a cocktail shaker with a handful of ice cubes and shake for about 20 seconds until the shaker is extremely cold to the touch.

② Strain into the glasses and top up with the dry sparkling wine.

③ To garnish, cut two thin shavings of lemon zest, twist to release the oils, then add one to each glass.

EQUIPMENT

* cocktail shaker
* 2 coupe glasses
* juicer
* fine-mesh strainer

DARK CHOCOLATE RASPBERRY DREAM

MAKES 2 SERVINGS

I first created this cocktail to celebrate Easter when I was appearing on a UK TV show called *Love your Weekend with Alan Titchmarsh*, hosted by one of the country's favourite TV presenters, where the drink was described by Alan as 'outrageous'. We all go a little overboard with chocolate at this time of year, but it doesn't always have to be egg-shaped. Put the eggs down and try this fruity chocolate beauty. The combination of raspberry and dark chocolate is just divine.

Freeze-dried raspberries float better than real raspberries and taste really vibrant. For a non-alcoholic version, replace the raspberry liqueur with Berry Syrup (see page 21), and make sure that the dark (bittersweet) chocolate you use is not too sweet.

PROPORTIONS

1 part milk

1 part cream

2 parts raspberry liqueur

INGREDIENTS

100ml/4fl oz whole (full-fat) milk

100ml/4fl oz double (heavy) cream

35g/1½oz dark (bittersweet) chocolate, shaved, grated (shredded) or finely chopped

200ml/7fl oz raspberry liqueur

6 freeze-dried (or fresh) raspberries

handful of ice cubes (optional)

EQUIPMENT

- saucepan
- whisk
- wooden spoon or spatula
- sterilised container
- 2 martini glasses

METHOD

① Pour the milk and cream into a saucepan, then add the chocolate.

② Heat gently, whisking constantly until the mixture simmers and the chocolate has melted. You now have a delicious hot chocolate.

③ Allow the mixture to cool slightly for 5 minutes or so, then pour in the raspberry liqueur and stir.

④ Allow to cool to room temperature, then pour into a clean, sterilised container and refrigerate for at least an hour. (If making ahead of time, it will last in the fridge for 3 days – just shake before drinking.)

⑤ If you are in a rush, once the drink has cooled for 10 minutes, pour into a cocktail shaker with a handful of ice cubes and shake for about 20 seconds until the shaker is extremely cold to the touch.

⑥ Pour into martini glasses and garnish with the freeze-dried raspberries.

BASIL BALL BASH

MAKES 2 SERVINGS

Being someone who grew up on '80s and '90s music, I follow a lot of pop stars on social media. I was really happy to discover that New Kids on the Block band member Danny Wood is a real food and drink fanatic. We've been following each other online for a while now and I was captivated by a creation I saw him make on Instagram. I love basil as a flavour in the warm summer months and I think it's very much an underrated herb in cocktails. I asked him if I could include it in the book and he was happy for me to share it. This is the perfect cocktail to listen to your old vinyl to. It really is 'The Right Stuff'.

And note, the reason it's called a Basil Ball Bash is that Danny likes to use one piece of spherical ice in a lowball glass to add to the individual drinking pleasure of this drink. You can buy ice cube moulds to make globe-like ice and it's really worth it.

PROPORTIONS

6 parts vodka

1 part lime juice

2 parts Simple Sugar Syrup

INGREDIENTS

16–20 large basil leaves

150ml/5fl oz vodka

25g/1fl oz fresh lime juice

50ml/2fl oz Simple Sugar Syrup (see page 17)

few handfuls of ice cubes

splash of soda water

EQUIPMENT

- cocktail shaker
- muddler or a wooden spoon or rolling pin
- 2 lowball glasses
- juicer
- fine-mesh strainer

TO GARNISH

large ball of ice

6 slices of cucumber

2 wedges of lime

4 basil leaves

METHOD

① Place the basil leaves in a cocktail shaker and muddle them. Add the vodka, lime juice and Simple Sugar Syrup to the cocktail shaker with a few handfuls of ice and shake for about 20 seconds until the shaker is extremely cold to the touch.

② Put the ball of ice in each glass and strain in the cocktail. Top up with a splash of soda water, if you like.

PINEAPPLE SMASH

MAKES 2 SERVINGS

I adore pineapple and all of its fruity charms. When something is so beautifully fragrant and sweet, I find I want to corrupt it with heat, especially in the summer! Introducing pineapple to red chilli feels a bit like sitting the good kid next to the naughty kid at school, but hey – opposites attract. This daring combo works on so many levels – the addition of basil, white rum and lime juice make this cocktail taste like a flavour explosion. This refreshing treat will heat you up while cooling you down!

INGREDIENTS

100ml/4fl oz white rum

½ red chilli

8 basil leaves

200ml/7fl oz pineapple juice

50ml/2fl oz fresh lime juice

1 egg white

2 large handfuls of ice cubes

dry sparkling wine (optional)

PROPORTIONS

2 parts white rum

4 parts pineapple juice

1 part lime juice

TO GARNISH

shavings of lime zest

EQUIPMENT STIRRER

- cocktail shaker
- muddler
- juicer
- 2 lowball glasses (or highball with sparking wine)
- fine-mesh strainer

METHOD

① Put the rum, chilli and basil leaves in a cocktail shaker and muddle. Add the pineapple juice, lime juice and egg white and shake for about 10 seconds. Add a handful of ice cubes and then shake for about 20 seconds more until the shaker is extremely cold to the touch.

② Fill the glasses with ice and strain the cocktail into the glasses.

③ To garnish, cut two thin shavings of lime zest, twist to release the oils, then add one to each glass.

④ For a longer drink, and to make it a little more like a Flirtini, top up with dry sparkling wine.

THE NEON YUZU

MAKES 2 SERVINGS

The tastes of Japan are as evocative and as exciting as the varied sites you see when you visit this amazing country. One of my most vivid memories of Japan is of seeing the bright lights of Osaka and tasting the incredible flavour of yuzu, a tiny citrus fruit with a summery character all of its own. With these memories in mind, I wanted to create a cocktail that sums up the rush you get when you experience Japanese night life ... And yuzu sake is the perfect drink to accompany your own karaoke party too!

PROPORTIONS

4 parts yuzu sake

2 parts vodka

1 part Citrus Syrup

INGREDIENTS

200ml/7fl oz yuzu sake

100 ml/4fl oz vodka

50ml/2fl oz Citrus Syrup (see page 18)

1 egg white

handful of ice cubes

TO GARNISH

2 sprigs of Thai basil

METHOD

① Put the yuzu sake, vodka, citrus syrup and egg white into a cocktail shaker and shake for about 10 seconds. Add a handful of ice cubes and shake for about 20 seconds more until the shaker is extremely cold to the touch. Pour into Champagne coupes.

② Hold the end of the basil stems between your thumb and forefinger, hit them on a chopping board 5 times to release the aromas. Garnish the top of each cocktail with the bruised basil.

EQUIPMENT

- cocktail shaker
- 2 Champagne coupes

WHISKY MAC +

MAKES 2 SERVINGS

This classic from the turn of the 20th century was created by Colonel Hector 'Fighting Mac' MacDonald using the warm and fiery flavour combination of whisky and ginger. Ginger wine isn't something you see every day, but it is a great accompaniment to Scotch. These days, the wine to whisky ratio often differs according to taste, but for me, this is the perfect combination.

This cocktail is great for sipping around the campfire as the nights draw in. But what does the + mean? I add a dash of lime juice to cut through the heat – this isn't traditional, it's just a modern way of trying the drink.

This drink is also great at room temperature. Or try heating it up to warm you on a cold night.

PROPORTIONS

6 parts whisky

6 parts ginger wine

1 part lime juice

INGREDIENTS

2 handfuls of ice cubes

150ml/5fl oz whisky

150ml/5fl oz ginger wine

25ml/1fl oz fresh lime juice

TO GARNISH

2 wedges of lime

METHOD

① Put a handful of ice cubes into a jug. Add the whisky, ginger wine and lime juice and stir. Put ice cubes into both glasses and strain the cocktail into the glasses.

② Garnish with a wedge of lime on the rim of each glass.

EQUIPMENT

- glass jug or pitcher
- stirrer
- 2 lowball glasses
- fine-mesh strainer
- juicer

APPLEVINI

MAKES 2 SERVINGS

One of the greatest seasonal events of the year for a fruit-lover like me is the apple harvest, when trees offer up their sweet fruit. But there's way more to the humble apple than just being one of your five-a-day.

I love the zing of apple cider vinegar. It's not just something to use in salad dressings, it can be a fabulous and invigorating cocktail ingredient. An Appletini is a wonderful celebration of apples but my Applevini takes the bright orchard flavour hit of an apple-based cocktail to a new dimension. You can make it for two or it's also great made for a larger group of friends to enjoy at parties in the fall.

PROPORTIONS

4 parts vodka

4 parts triple sec

4 parts cloudy apple juice

1 part apple cider vinegar

INGREDIENTS

handful of ice cubes

100ml/4fl oz vodka

100ml/4fl oz triple sec

100ml/4fl oz cloudy apple juice

25 ml/1fl oz apple cider vinegar

TO GARNISH

1 apple, cut into discs

METHOD

① Put the ice in a cocktail shaker and add all the liquid ingredients. Shake for about 20 seconds until the shaker is extremely cold to the touch.

② Pour into the martini glasses and garnish with a disc of your favourite local apple.

EQUIPMENT

- cocktail shaker
- 2 martini glasses

FOR 6 PEOPLE

You can also make this in batch quantities.

3 handfuls of ice cubes

300ml/10fl oz vodka

300ml/10fl oz triple sec

300ml/10fl oz cloudy apple juice

75ml/2½fl oz apple cider vinegar

① Put the ice and all the liquid ingredients into a jug and stir gently until blended and cold.

② Pour into martini glasses and garnish with apple, as previous page.

SPICED PUMPKIN BELLINI

MAKES 2 SERVINGS

I get really excited when pumpkin comes into season. It's not just for carving – there are great-tasting pumpkins available all over the place once summer is far behind us. This cocktail is a seasonal take on the Bellini but rather than using peach purée, this one uses pumpkin purée. It also has a delicious spiced-sugar rim and is perfect for Halloween parties.

PROPORTIONS

1 part pumpkin purée

2 parts sparkling wine

FOR THE PUMPKIN PURÉE

200g/7oz pumpkin flesh, cubed (or you can use squash)

100ml/4fl oz cloudy apple juice

3 tbsp Ginger Syrup (see page 19) or 1 tsp ground ginger

½ tsp ground cinnamon

FOR THE SUGARED RIM

1 tsp ground ginger

1 tsp ground cinnamon

1 tsp caster (superfine) sugar

FOR THE COCKTAILS

130ml/4½fl oz pumpkin purée

260ml/9fl oz dry sparkling wine

TO GARNISH

2 physalis (Cape gooseberries)

EQUIPMENT

- saucepan
- fine-mesh strainer
- blender or food processor
- ramekin
- plate

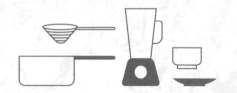

METHOD

① To make the purée, put the pumpkin cubes in a saucepan, just cover with water and bring to the boil. Reduce the heat and simmer for 15 minutes until tender. Drain and leave to cool.

② Blitz in a blender with the apple juice, the ginger syrup and ground cinnamon until smooth (I do it for 40 seconds). If you don't have a blender, use a potato or a fork to create the purée.

③ Set aside to cool until it reaches room temperature. This will store in the fridge for 5 days, or it will freeze for 3 months.

④ To prepare the sugared rim, mix together the spices and sugar and put on a small plate. Put a little sparkling wine in a ramekin or small bowl. Dip the rim of the glasses in the sparkling wine and then immediately into the spice mix so the sugar and spice sticks to the rim. Stand the glasses upright.

⑤ Put the measured pumpkin purée in a small jug, pour in the dry sparkling wine and stir gently, then strain into Champagne flutes. Garnish each glass with a physalis.

EQUIPMENT

- small glass jug
- stirrer
- 2 Champagne flutes

GINGER JINGLE

MAKES 2 SERVINGS

Ginger has many feathers to its cap – it's invigorating, hot and yet feels comforting too. I love ginger as an addition to so many food and drink recipes. Here, I'm letting it take centre stage in a drink that will excite you throughout your winter celebrations. If you'd like a sweeter cocktail, add a teaspoon of Ginger Syrup (see page 19) to each glass, stir and serve.

PROPORTIONS

6 parts ginger ale

2 parts dry white vermouth

1 part bourbon

1 part lime juice

TO GARNISH

2 shavings of lime zest

10 frozen cranberries

INGREDIENTS

2 handfuls of ice cubes

300ml/10fl oz ginger ale

100ml/4fl oz dry white vermouth

50ml/2fl oz bourbon

50ml/2fl oz fresh lime juice

METHOD

① Put a handful of ice cubes in a jug. Add the ginger ale, vermouth, bourbon and lime juice and stir gently.

② Fill the glasses with ice, then strain in the cocktail.

③ To garnish, cut two thin shavings of lime zest, twist to release the oils, then add on to each glass. Add half the frozen cranberries to each drink and let them scatter throughout. These jewels of red will give the drink a festive look.

EQUIPMENT

- glass jug or pitcher
- juicer
- stirrer
- 2 collins glasses
- fine-mesh strainer

FROSTY THE MELTING SNOWMAN

MAKES 2 SERVINGS

Winter is the time of year when we can truly have fun with our food and drink. Kids love to get creative, so this creation is perfect for getting them involved. So, when any of us get the urge to make a snowman but there's no snow, don't worry because I am about to introduce you to a snowman (or should that be snowperson?) who will bring joy to the season in an extremely tasty way.

FOR THE SORBET

1 lemon

200g/7oz caster (superfine) sugar

200ml/7fl oz water

3 lemons

FOR THE COCKTAILS

4 scoops of sorbet

100ml/3fl oz limoncello or citrus drink (still traditional lemonade works nicely)

TO GARNISH

liquorice strands or an unwound wheel of liquorice (for the scarf)

4 currants (for the eyes)

2 pointed slices of orange peel (for the nose)

FOR THE SORBET

- vegetable peeler
- saucepan
- wooden spoon
- juicer
- freezable container

TO MAKE THE SORBET

① Use a vegetable peeler to remove the zest of the lemon, making sure that you don't take off too much of the white pith (as this could make your mixture bitter).

② Put the sugar, water and lemon zest in a saucepan over a low heat, stirring occasionally, until the sugar has dissolved. Bring to the boil, then reduce the heat and simmer for 5 minutes.

③ Remove from the heat and leave to cool. Take out the lemon zest.

④ Meanwhile, juice the lemons. Add the juice to the cooled mixture.

⑤ Pour the mixture into an ice cream machine and churn until frozen. Or put into a freezable container with lid and put in the freezer. Stir the mixture once every hour for 4–5 hours until frozen. The sorbet will last in the freezer for up to 2 months.

TO MAKE THE COCKTAILS

① Heat the liquid – either limoncello or non-alcoholic alternative – in a saucepan until steaming but do not allow it to boil. Set aside.

② Put 2 large scoops of sorbet at the bottom of each glass to create the body. Add smaller scoops on top to create the head. Drape the liquorice around the neck to form the scarf. Add the currant eyes and the orange peel nose. Pour the hot liquid over the snowmen and watch them melt. Using a spoon, eat the sorbet, or drink once totally melted!

FOR THE COCKTAILS

- ice cream scoop
- 2 lowball glasses

MULLED WINE

MAKES 8 SERVINGS

This is a warming classic, but the great thing about it is that you don't have to stick to the rules. Just like when you make a cheese sauce with all the cheese board cheese left over from Christmas Day, you can use pretty much whatever spirits you want in your mulled wine. So although I have given proportions for this recipe, as long as you get the basic recipe sorted (red wine, spices and sweetener) you can play around with the rest to your heart's content – why not have a rummage around your drinks cabinet? Traditionally the drink is made with sugar, but I think maple syrup gives it real character.

If you'd like to add a dash of fresh acidity, squeeze a lemon into your drink after you've poured it. This way, you get your hit of citrus even if others don't want it. You can also add 200ml/7fl oz of fresh orange juice to give it a Sangria-like twist! And if you're in a warm climate at Christmas, let it cool down to room temperature or even serve over ice.

PROPORTIONS

7½ parts red wine

1 part triple sec

1 part brandy

1 part maple syrup

INGREDIENTS

750ml/25fl oz (1 bottle) medium-bodied dry red wine (an easy-drinking Italian red does the trick nicely)

100ml/7fl oz triple sec

100ml/7fl oz brandy

100ml/7fl oz maple syrup (you could use honey or 50g/2oz caster (superfine) sugar, if you prefer

1 orange, sliced

2 cinnamon sticks

2 star anise

6 cloves

EQUIPMENT

- large saucepan or casserole (Dutch oven)
- 8 heatproof glasses or mugs
- ladle

METHOD

① Put all the ingredients in a large saucepan, cover and heat gently until the mixture is steaming but not boiling. Keep it on a low heat and let it stay at that temperature for at least 20 minutes.

② Reduce the heat slightly and keep it warm. Ladle out the drink into heatproof mugs with handles. Use the floating spices and fruit as garnish and feel free to add more cinnamon or star anise as garnish, if you like.

COCKTAIL-TIME SNACKS

Eating and drinking go hand in hand and there's rarely a time where snacks aren't called for when sipping cocktails, so here are a few ideas for you to snack on while you whet your whistle. Remember, they are only snacks so they will provide you with a few bites of loveliness to accompany your favourite drinks. They're all relatively easy, can all be made in advance and the recipes are easy to double up if you would like more.

Just a bit of housekeeping: make sure you wash any fresh ingredients you use. And don't use sharp knives or cookers while under the influence of cocktails!

HUMMUS

MAKES 4 SERVINGS

This is my all-time favourite pre-dinner snack. It always gets me in the mood for an exquisite cocktail and I never tire of it. You can add so many flavours to hummus – roasted pepper, pesto, caramelised onions … to name a few, but the classic version is still my favourite. I've tried so many times to get the recipe right and I've never been happier with it. I love dipping crudités in my hummus (organic carrots and peppers are so crunchy and full of flavour) but toasted pitta is also great. Good old crisps or potato chips are pretty amazing too. But you can dip whatever you like in it!

INGREDIENTS

400g/14oz can of chickpeas (garbanzos)

100ml/4fl oz extra virgin olive oil

2 garlic cloves (peeled)

juice and zest of 1 lemon

4 tbsp tahini

25ml/1fl oz chickpea water (aquafaba)

salt and freshly ground black pepper

pinch of paprika

TO SERVE

crudités

toasted pitta bread

tortilla chips

EQUIPMENT

- juicer
- blender or food processor
- spatula

METHOD

① Drain the chickpeas and set the water aside. Tip into the bowl of a food processor with the garlic, lemon juice, lemon zest, tahini, 80ml (3fl oz) of the oil and 2 tablespoons of the chickpea water. Blitz for a minute or so or until almost smooth.

② Scrape the sides of the bowl with a spatula in order to bring in any of the mixture that hasn't blended, add two more spoons of chickpea water, a large pinch of salt and a few grinds of black pepper then blitz again for around 2 minutes or until the hummus is as smooth as you like. (I like mine to have a bit of texture, but if you like it really smooth, just keep blitzing!)

③ Taste and adjust seasoning if necessary. Transfer into a serving bowl if serving immediately or store in a clean sealable container if making in advance. Before serving, if desired, drizzle the remaining oil over the hummus along with a pinch of paprika. I love to serve mine with crunchy vegetable crudités, toasted pitta bread and tortilla chips.

GUACAMOLE

MAKES 4 SERVINGS

For years, I was never a fan of guacamole. I found it mushy and bland. But as everybody else I was spending time with seemed to love the stuff, I felt that I had to learn to appreciate it, so I started making it from scratch. I found that it was actually really easy to make and so much tastier than the versions I'd previously found in supermarkets. But not only this, I discovered that I loved the flavours. It was no longer one-dimensional, it now tasted vibrant and interesting. I hope you love this recipe as much as I do.

INGREDIENTS

2 ripe avocados

1 lime

1 tomato

1 birdseye chilli

1 large garlic clove

½ tsp smoked paprika

sea salt

handful of coriander (cilantro)

TO SERVE

lightly salted fried tortilla chips

EQUIPMENT

- bowl
- kitchen towel
- masher

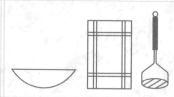

METHOD

① Halve the avocados by running a sharp knife around them. Twist and pull the halves apart. Use the knife to remove the stone by hitting the stone with the sharp side of the knife and twisting it. It should come out easily. Scoop out the avocado flesh with a dessert spoon and put into a bowl. Squeeze the juice of the lime over the avocado flesh.

② Chop the tomato into even pieces about 5mm/¼in square. Put the tomato pieces on top of a sheet of paper towel and place another sheet on top. Leave for 2 minutes so that the towels soak up the excess moisture.

③ Halve the chilli, remove the seeds and finely chop. (You want to make sure the chilli is in very small pieces, so it distributes evenly into the guacamole.) Add the chilli to the bowl.

④ Remove the paper-like skin of the garlic clove, then cut the clove into quarters. Finely slice the pieces and add them to the bowl.

⑤ Put the tomato pieces in the bowl and add the paprika and a large pinch of salt. Roughly chop the coriander and mash all the ingredients together but don't break up the avocado too much – it's much nicer when it's slightly chunky. Taste and season with more salt or paprika if necessary, give the guacamole one final stir and serve with lightly salted fried tortilla chips or anything you fancy dipping!

SPICY NUTS

MAKES 8 SERVINGS

A flavoursome salty nut is the perfect accompaniment to cocktails. I love to use cashews, peanuts, hazelnuts (filberts), macadamia nuts and walnuts, but alternatively you can buy nuts already mixed instead of creating your own mix. These can be served warm from the pan or cold from the cupboard. The great thing is that they will last for three weeks when stored in a clean sealed container.

This recipe can use any nuts you want and any dried herb or spice you may have in your cupboard. Now I'm happy with the basic recipe, I tend to chuck in whatever I have and whatever needs using. Just remember, it's easy to forget you have nuts and dried seasonings in the cupboard until well after their use-by date, so make sure you check the dates before you partake!

INGREDIENTS

1 tbsp vegetable oil

200g/7oz unsalted mixed nuts (this should cover the base of a large frying pan)

1 tbsp dried mixed herbs

2 tsp dried chilli flakes

1 tsp five-spice powder

1 tsp unsmoked paprika

1 tsp garlic powder

1 tsp onion salt

1 tsp sea salt

EQUIPMENT

- frying pan (skillet)
- spatula

METHOD

① Heat the oil in a large frying pan over a medium heat for around 1 minute until hot but not smoking. Add the nuts and stir so that they are all coated in the oil. Add the dry ingredients and stir again so that the nuts are evenly coated. Leave for a minute to let the nuts toast – you should hear them sizzle.

② After a minute, stir again – or toss them in the pan if you're feeling confident! Leave for a further minute, or until you are happy that they are toasted but not burning. Take off the heat, decant into a bowl and leave for 5 minutes before serving.

CREAM CHEESE TORTILLA SWIRLS WITH SALMON OR HAM

MAKES 2 SERVINGS

Cream cheese is the most wonderful ingredient to use when creating nibbles. Yes, it's great on savoury crackers but you can do so much more with it, with very little effort.

I love these little bite-sized versions of a cream cheese wrap. They are equally delicious with either smoked salmon or ham, so the choice is yours.

INGREDIENTS

1 tortilla wrap or thin pancake (about 25cm/10in in diameter)

30g/1oz soft cream cheese

a few grinds of black pepper

handful of washed rocket or baby spinach leaves with the stems removed (around 10g/¼oz)

A CHOICE TO SERVE

4 slices of thin ham (about 100g/4oz)

4 slices smoked salmon

squeeze of lemon juice

METHOD

① Lay the wrap on a chopping board and cut into a square by taking off the four edges of the circle. Save the cut edges for later.

② Spread half the cream cheese on the square wrap, making sure that it reaches the edges. Grind a little pepper over the cream cheese. Layer the rocket or spinach on the cream cheese. (They will lie flat easily as the cheese acts like an edible glue.)

③ Layer the ham or smoked salmon on top. If you're using smoked salmon squeeze a little lemon juice on once the fish is in place. Spread the rest of the cream cheese on top, once again making sure it reaches the edges.

EQUIPMENT
• cocktail sticks (toothpicks)

④ Now it's time to roll the wrap. Lift the edge that is nearest to you away from the chopping board and roll the wrap up tightly. If it's rolled tight, it will keep its shape once cut.

⑤ Once rolled, the wrap will resemble a sausage. Cut off either end so that the ends are neat, making sure you taste the edges you've cut off – we don't want to waste anything.

⑥ Cut the wrap in half and then cut each half into three. You will now have six rolls. Pierce each roll with a cocktail stick so that it runs through the whole roll. This will enable them to keep their shape. Fan your rolls on a plate and go make a fabulous cocktail!

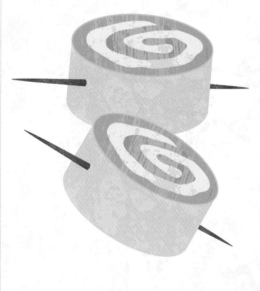

TOMATO BRUSCETTA

MAKES 4 SERVINGS

The flavour of good-quality ripe tomatoes is an example of how great mother nature can be. The simplicity of good produce will make your snacks incredible. I love putting this delicious juicy tomato mixture atop crispy sourdough to make the ultimate Italianesque cocktail-friendly snack.

INGREDIENTS

400g/14oz tomatoes (use whatever variety is in season, that you like and you can get your hands on)

½ red onion, finely diced

3 garlic cloves

handful of fresh basil leaves (around 10), roughly chopped

100ml/4fl oz extra virgin olive oil

200g/7oz sourdough bread, sliced into 8 equal portions

salt and freshly ground black pepper

METHOD

① Chop the tomatoes into even pieces about 5mm/¼in square. Put the tomato pieces on top of a sheet of paper towel and place another sheet on top. Leave for 2 minutes so that the towels soak up the excess moisture.

② Remove the skin of the garlic cloves, put the red onion in a bowl then chop 1 clove of garlic and add to the bowl. Also add the basil and tomatoes and mix all the ingredients together. Add 50ml/2fl oz of olive oil, season with salt and pepper to taste, stir and set to one side. This can be made a day in advance and kept in the fridge. If you do this, make sure you bring it to room temperature before you serve as the flavours will be fuller. You may also need to drain a little liquid from the tomatoes as more comes out over time.

③ Toast the sourdough bread until the desired crispiness has been reached and let it cool for 1 minute, then remove from the toaster.

EQUIPMENT

- toaster
- presentation board or plate
- large bowl

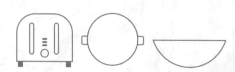

④ Take the remaining garlic cloves and rub them over the slices of toasted sourdough bread (they will grate on the texture of the bread and wear away) then drizzle the remaining olive oil over each slice.

⑤ Arrange the bread on a presentation board or plate and gently spoon on your tomato mixture. Once you're ready to eat be careful as you pick them up as the tomato can topple!

HARISSA PRAWNS

MAKES 2 SERVINGS

Nibbling on seafood with a drink in hand reminds me of being on holiday, so making a vacation-style dish at home can make you feel like you're on a mini-break, even when you're not! Prawns are delicious, juicy bites of joy and are so easy to cook. Using raw King prawns will give you the tastiest shellfish treat – and they're so easy to find in shops and markets, whether frozen or fresh. Do try to avoid using cooked prawns as when they are reheated they lose their soft, juicy texture and can feel a little rubbery in the mouth. If you have no choice, add them at the last minute, just to heat through.

Harissa is a beautiful hot paste that contains varieties of chilli peppers, garlic and spices. Strongly associated with Tunisia, there are many versions of harissa across many North African regions. Jars of harissa are readily available in shops and markets all over the globe, so find one you like and crack on! I love using rose harissa, which has rose petals added. Don't worry – it doesn't taste of Turkish delight, it just has a gentle floral note that tempers the heat and complements shellfish perfectly.

INGREDIENTS

12 raw king prawns (or any large prawns)

1 tsp olive oil

2 tbsp harissa (or rose harissa)

5 or 6 fresh coriander leaves (optional)

EQUIPMENT

- spatula
- frying pan (skillet)
- cocktail sticks (toothpicks)
- small bowl (a terracotta bowl works nicely)

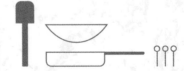

METHOD

① Take the prawns out of the fridge or freezer and allow them to reach room temperature. Put the oil in a frying pan and place the pan over medium heat.

② Put the prawns in a bowl and add the harissa. Stir until the prawns are evenly coated with the paste.

③ After a minute, the oil should have heated up to the correct temperature. Add the prawns gently and make sure

they are all touching the hot base of the pan. After about 1 minute they should have turned pink on the underside. Turn them over and leave to cook on the other side for a further minute. Make sure the prawns are pink all over and hot throughout. Take off the heat and put the prawns in your bowl of choice.

④ Roughly chop the coriander and sprinkle over the top. Eat with cocktail sticks in one hand and a fabulous cocktail in the other!

ABOUT ANDY CLARKE

Andy Clarke is one of the 21st century's most exciting voices in the world of food and drink.

Having travelled across the globe working as a food, drink and travel television producer and director, Andy started to use his vibrant writing style and lively personality to communicate his life-long love of bringing people together through food and drink.

Andy's food and drink recommendations have gained attention and (much to the dismay of his friends and family) he is now happy to call himself a 'professional eater and drinker'!

Andy is at his happiest when sharing his love of all things sippable and edible on television, through social media, in print and online, and by hosting festivals and events.

Throughout his career, Andy has worked with some of the world's greatest chefs and drinks experts, he regularly judges for international food and drinks awards and is a consultant to the hospitality industry.

ACKNOWLEDGEMENTS

I raise a glass to every person who has ever brought a smile to my face. To my mum and dad for raising me to see the good in everyone, for encouraging me to appreciate good food & drink and for being happy to let me be who I happend to be. To my husband, Alan O'Shea, for allowing me to enjoy every second of life even more than I already did before we met in 2005. To the people in the hospitality and TV industries who I have worked with and who have given me the confidence to work hard and believe in myself. To the chefs who have helped me to engage my inquisitive palate and enter the international food and drink industry with pride. To the drinks experts who made me realise I might know what I'm talking about. To my publisher, Kate Pollard, for believing in me and my love of drinking, and to all the team at Welbeck who have helped me put this book in front of you. To all the friends who allowed me to test my cocktail creations on them, and most of all, to you for picking up this book and reading this far. Let's hope that we can 'sip happy' for the rest of our lives.

First published in 2022 by OH Editions
This edition published in 2024 by OH
An Imprint of HEADLINE PUBLISHING GROUP

1

Cataloguing in Publication Data is available from the
British Library

Hardback ISBN 978-1-91431-735-4

Printed and bound in China by RR Donnelley

HEADLINE PUBLISHING GROUP
An Hachette UK Company
Carmelite House
50 Victoria Embankment
London EC4Y 0DZ

Publisher: Kate Pollard
Editor: Wendy Hobson
Designers: Evi-O.Studio | Susan Le & Wilson Leung
Illustrators: Evi-O.Studio | Susan Le, Emi Chiba
& Kait Polkinghorne
Production controller: Arlene Alexander

www.headline.co.uk
www.hachette.co.uk